Mental Anarchy

Tourette's Syndrome and American Dystopia

ANTHONY MORITT

Copyright © 2015 Anthony Moritt

All rights reserved. No part of this publication may be reproduced, distributed, or transmitted in any form or by any means, including photocopying, recording, or other electronic or mechanical methods, without the prior written permission of the author, except in the case of brief quotations embodied in critical reviews and certain other non-commercial uses permitted by copyright law unless document receives visible attribution and author notified beforehand. For permission requests, write to the publisher, addressed "Attention: Permissions Coordinator," at the email address below.

david@dmgworldwideconsulting.com

Ordering Information:

Quantity sales. Special discounts are available on quantity purchases by corporations, associations, and others. For details, contact the publisher at the address above.

Published in the United States of America
Cover art by Juan Gonzalez

ISBN: 1518653529

ISBN-13: 978-1518653520

DEDICATION

I tried to be sardonic, as I always am, but I would be remiss to not dedicate my first project to my beloved mother. Love you mom.

CONTENTS

Foreword	vii
Reacting to Suspicion	Pg 1
The Triad	Pg 7
Early Childhood	Pg 11
Schools and Teachers	Pg 20
Into the Fog	Pg 32
Probability	Pg 40
Drugs and Alcohol	Pg 47
Money, Authority, Government, God, and Liquor	Pg 58
On Detestable People	Pg 74
The Dating Chapter	Pg 98
Dating Part II	Pg 107
Dating Part III	Pg 118
Final Address	Pg 138
About the Author	Pg 146

FOREWORD

This is the best possible evening to begin serious productivity on this book. The last evening has been a torrent of upheaving emotions unseen since the loss of my beloved Pop Pop. I lost the girl I thought I loved more than anything, leading to an initial wave of massive depression. Once more, on October 12th, 2013 I broke free. I drank a bit, smoked some pot, hung out with what little support network I have allotted myself; even took a beautiful Mexican citizen on a date I couldn't have possibly afforded had I been betrothed to that parasite.

Last night I found out she is seeing someone.

Just in time! I get to return to grad school to face down the polarizing eyes of an atrociously severed relationship. She makes love to him, confides in him, and he fears me. Another self-inflicted conflict ensued. Besides the fact that watching someone completely move on from three years shared and within a month is sleeping around being absolutely torturous, I reacted in a way that was non-threatening but thoroughly brutal. First I cried starting at 10:08PM before sleeping with an old classmate, likely snoring through the evening, making an exquisite breakfast, and winding up here.

Why does any of this matter? Because with Tourette's Syndrome and its "sister disorders" OCD, ADHD, and others questions of morality, sexual deviance, and intoxication is an entirely different ballgame than your average gentleman within the chains of an identity crisis.

I will never look at the same thing from your perspective or anyone else's. We are unique; we are intelligent, athletic, beautiful, talented, and misunderstood by society. My willingness to accept responsibility for the things I said and the things I did which caused a cataclysmic break-up was enough to atone for my sins. She can move on, and I can too. If one more blonde girl at a neighboring bar stool asks me if I curse regularly I might just tell her to fuck off and blame it on my TS. Realistically, my opinions are my own and if I want to curse someone it is damn well my own volition. Some politically correct parents may cast aside this book like a grimoire of pure evil. A few

Protestants here, some leftists there, will all come to fear what they may learn. Yet, this book is not meant to be a tome of sin augmented by the riveting irregularity that is TS.

What makes Tourette's such a roller coaster from Hell is in my case it manifests in my emotions far more than my tics themselves. I still have those embarrassing, joint dislocating, decades of suffering arm extensions, head bobs, and a few other classic tics. What sets us apart is every thought we have ever had has been brought upon by the influence of Tourette's Syndrome. While the disorder does not grip me, it surely taints (or clarifies) the looking glass of my worldview in many ways.

It was never an easy road. My first creation is not one of debauchery and pessimism. It is a book designed to teach people from both my experiences with myself and others how to understand and better comprehend the rigors of what they are facing. This book might never be children's reading, nor a schoolyard favorite. This may never get me on Oprah, or stamps of approval from the Catholic church. It will get me glances of questionable favor, accusations of rabble rousing, possible PR disasters and maybe a few gold digging harlots should I be fortunate enough to become successful.

Tourette's has an iron fist and a gorilla glue grip,

and even though it wins a few battles, it never won the war. It's the same way with people, whether it is a battle against or alongside someone, whether it is malignant or merely competitive. We can't win all of them, but the big picture is most important.

There won't just be talks about drugs, and sex, and violence, and argumentativeness. Yes, concerned parent, I will help you and your afflicted child learn how to manage themselves personally from the assaults of thought, the teeming obsessions, and the challenging transitions in life, in the classroom, in romance, and in every other facet imaginable. Publishing this book will be the first time my parents find out a lot of things about me. Whatever throes of criticism I have to endure, I will gladly shoulder the chastising. This is more important than me, or my wallet, or my ego. This is about helping people achieve a greater self-awareness of their condition, while taking some of the mistakes and triumphs of my young life and building upon their own.

Together we are going to cover every visceral, politically incorrect subject. Every incorrigible moment in my life, every mirthful and damning experience, everything that made my life so eventful, comes out on these pages. Instead of this being a strange man's testimonial, I am going to parlay my experiences and understanding of my condition to convey hope and some semblance of a linguistic boost to the world and reveal that everything that happens is a lesson and every victory is to be savored!

Read along, laugh with me, cringe at some of these dastardly tales, but most of all take it deeper than face value. Don't judge a book by its cover, and don't judge my words as a mere story.

REACTING TO SUSPICION

My personal story had me doing a tic that stuck with me from day one. It normally manifests today only in small doses and almost every time I meet a new girl and have to explain to her why I look like such an oddball. Obviously, years ago there were fewer answers and far fewer people aware of Tourette's Syndrome (TS) so head bobbing like a cockatoo after a Red Bull binge was a strange sight indeed.

Later, I was typing up homework and went off on our first computer with Windows 3.1 striking the backslash and control buttons along with backspace, typing some cryptic alien language with a linguistic pattern that only Ramses II could understand. I had an ability to type at any speed so the precision in which I struck the keys was remarkable. Clearly something was off. While today it serves as a comedic memory, then it was just short of a possession. Certain disorders don't have the alarming portrayal as Forrest Gump in his braces or Leonardo DiCaprio's character in that Gilbert Grape film. By the way, I recommend that movie if you're a cinema masochist and love to suffer.

If you've heard of Tourette's, we can thank the TSA (the Tourette's Syndrome Association. Not the people you'll find in the airport) and their comprehensive efforts to explain the disorder to the public. Please understand that Tourette's Syndrome is a significant challenge well beyond the realms of ADHD. There is much ado about the "Triad" later, but while it is a real endeavor, people with Tourette's will be special in their own way. Those with Tourette's can look forward to having a unique personality but also a life where troubles can quickly become overwhelming.

It is important to understand that the initial onset of TS should not be treated as some "mystery" affliction. Early days, for those with TS, are fundamental in establishing vibes. In the past, I have struggled to comprehend why I cannot stop doing what I am doing. If each one of my chapters had one sentence among all of my long-winded linguistic arson to take to heart, this next one is that - paramount. Do not treat those with TS as if they are any different. If a guy gets his legs blown off or is autistic, you obviously have to take alternative measures for treatment and understanding, but those of us with TS that are at least controllable can fit right in with the hordes of society. The biggest issue to address is psychological damage. People with TS may feel depressed, confused, and more than likely dissonant. I am not a freak, despite the societal reactions we may illicit. Not everyone unilaterally scream expletives. I wouldn't have written these words if this wasn't a unique and special challenge to everyone in their lives.

I have never met anyone with TS in my life that wasn't talented or proficient at something extraordinary. It's that six-year old who had no idea why he was bobbing his head but had a forehand that had Wimbledon calling. Or the lady in her thirties who was fearful of even dating and is now wedded and happier than ever. What about one of my best friends? His mom was instrumental in the local TSA organization in Broward County, Florida. The guy is a marvelous chef and possibly the most low-key and likable person I know. It doesn't matter, because we are not defined by our genetic code, but the content and loft of our character. Think of it not as a monkey on the back, or as Atlas bearing the weight of the world, but a small tote holding a bit of troubles that we carry onto the rocket ride we know as life.

When I was seven, my original questioning came from Doctor H, my pediatrician. Not only was he the most pleasant man in the world, but he also had Disney murals painted all over his walls and could even make an injection feel warm and fuzzy. As I sat there bobbing and weaving my migraine inflicted skull about, Dr. H. told my mother I should indeed see a neurologist about Tourette's Syndrome. Now keep in mind that the 21st Century is a luxury in comparison to 1997 or God forbid back when religion scorched everyone that looked silly. Of course, right after Dr. H. looked up my nose (proclaiming "Here's Mickey!" followed by Goofy and Donald Duck in either ear, with Minnie dwelling in my left nostril) and finished the regular check-up my growing body required, he made this fateful suggestion. The Doc showed no panic, but informed my mother, who then burst into hysterics. Why, you ask? Because she had no clue what Tourette's Syndrome was.

Previously mentioned was the TSA, which has blossomed into a major neurological research and advocacy organization. Thankfully the involvement of thousands of dedicated parents and a few terrific professionals boosted the organization and education about the disorder into prominence. Later, I'll talk about the educational portion of Tourette's and just how to survive the rigors of the scholastic arena with minimal struggles.

Some days I wake up and my thoughts take control of me. This morning which, is December 10th 2013, I awoke to thoughts of pure evil. And yet, while there are so many things for me to feel putrid bitterness about, I have to thank the stars that I was born with Tourette's and not another genetic disaster that could cripple or kill me before I turned ten. The road ahead is not an easy one, but it could be much, much worse. People need to learn not to attach titles to others. When someone says, "That's Anthony, the guy with Tourette's," I honestly want to throw an apple at their face. Why don't we say, "Oh that's Rob, he's a felon." Or "There's Kenny, the dude with the ego that outsizes his pecker?" We don't because we don't find it acceptable. Sure, the baggage is there, but so is yours, so is their friend's, and so is everyone else's.

The trouble begins with Tourette's, but it truly manifests with societal integration. Those with TS are not only a human, but sentinels, watchdogs, protectors, and advocates. Involvement in life is tantamount to successes in the public sphere. It is extremely important that those with TS follow what I have to say in chapters about co-ed mingling and the classroom. These are the two places where failure is highest. I have managed to succeed at mingling, but -

dramatically underachieved in the classroom by my own volition. Regardless, even if I do come off as a bad influence, I can help those with TS succeed where I failed. Read along, and understand that you are beginning an arduous journey that, when conquered, will allow peaks to be scaled that are not reachable by the simpletons of society.

THE TRIAD

Let me explain the terminology I will use throughout this book. The "Triad," hence, "tri," is what I call Tourette's Syndrome and its two "sister" disorders. This is where things get very interesting. By sister disorders I am speaking of Obsessive Compulsive Disorder and Attention Deficit Hyperactivity Disorder. These obviously are shortened to TS, OCD, and ADHD. While these disorders are funny to watch erroneously lampooned in immature films, these three in unison are a fearsome cocktail. They bounce off of each other. Imagine if every waking (and sleeping) thought in your mind was written into a sentence. Instead of the sentence being spelled perfectly in the English alphabet, every fifth letter is a Roman Numeral, while every third is in Sanskrit. Thus is the nature of the Triad, working in conjunction to create a wonderful blender-load of madness. To understand who I am, it is very important to know how they interact. For example, in my oh-so-moving chapter about losing my ex (admittedly I wrote that chapter first to absolve that nonsense, now that my condition has markedly improved as such) I explain that the Triad works together, but never positively. Ever notice how sometimes ex girlfriends hang out together? How their bond is only shared by their mutual hatred of you? I feel like the Triad is comparable to such a nefarious conglomerate. These three disorders in combination is like three strumpets getting together and scheming on how they can destroy the most of you at once.

This type of heinous action is exactly an adequate comparison to three Marxists planning a city, or the Legion of Doom preparing to assail the Super Friends (i.e, Marxists). This chapter does not need to be extraordinary in length. Just understand that a few things can contribute to increases in any symptom. Here are just a few: medication not taken on schedule, misappropriated prescriptions, increases in caffeine, alcohol or drugs, emotional highs and lows, stress or relaxation and many more.

The onset of hyperactivity can increase tics, creating an extremely stressful situation. Nothing is more obnoxious than having tics in an airport. Tics can blend with OCD, creating a musculoskeletal dependency called Tourettic OCD. Essentially it is an interaction with the outside world but instead of it satisfying a mental need it soothes a deep physical desire, much like a tic itself. Examples can be pressing buttons a certain way and with a certain frequency, or even touching people (which can get quite dicey).

I had a perfect example of that. While it sounds hysterically funny, in this version of America, I would likely face criminal charges. I had an extreme case of OCD in fourth grade where I would smack the rear ends of overweight girls in school. I never did it hard enough to cause pain, but it was for the satisfaction of that flat boom against my hand and the subsequent sound it made. Nowadays a kindergartener can get suspended for kissing his crush on the cheek, so only a soothsayer could explain what might've happened if I had not quickly hearkened the stern reprimand of my fourth grade science teacher.

While now it is funny and the girls in fourth grade found it funny too, this could get you in a shit load of trouble. Especially, as aforementioned, in a world where everyone's first priority is themselves this type of touch-based OCD can get you and your family in a bind. Nowadays there are news stories of the nanny state putting similarly strange children between a hard place and the sex offender registry before their baby teeth are gone. Be wary of the ramifications an overpowered state can have on your health.

Don't get into a frenzy, OCD can manifest in many ways. Strange past times and obsessions can grip someone at any time. This chapter was no fun, but it briefly explains the terminology. It is merely a quick descriptor. Good luck with the triad.

EARLY CHILDHOOD

There are two relative consistencies with Tourette's Syndrome: The overwhelming majority of cases are in boys, beginning between ages three and seven but clearly manifesting towards the tail end of elementary school. My closest friend for years was diagnosed in the same exact week as I was. He had a terrific mom (the aforementioned who started support in my county) and an angel for a sister. I have two overbearing (better than absent) but amazing parents. My parents made severe errors in judgment but we've maintained a healthy relationship all my life. A parent is not perfect. My support network was there.

My parents could write a book on how to manage me, but I'll do the best at replicating how they treated my early childhood. My mother and father chose a good time to divorce in July of 2007. I handled it very well. They were nice enough to break the news after I had enough time to get drunk and go absolutely bananas to end high school. When my Dad sat us down and told us he was leaving, my brother was pissed. I on the other hand was happy that the news they were breaking was just that and not the death of my chronically ill Nanny (RIP March 16, 2009). For every qualm and complaint and every bat-shit crazy tantrum I threw as a child, I am not mad about my parents. They are the best I could have ever hoped for.

I'm not a total idiot, and I never hit lows like jail time or narcotic rehab, but I did get pretty nasty. I was a little shit for most of my life, so I was able to become a tremendous preschool teacher thanks to my understanding of other little demons, but whereas they were products of neglectful and even abusive parenting, I was a victim of my own disability and perhaps the wealth I grew up around. Thankfully there are many places and gatherings, schools and communities, where you can find kids with the same issues. Often doctors will visit as they have patients in support groups, offering excellent advice to parents and teachers.

Don't let anyone tell you that you are any different from your classmates. While a disorder of the brain is treated as something more bizarre and dangerous to others than standard afflictions, this deviation cannot be the standard. Reclusion is a terrible enemy for those with Tourette's Syndrome. Thankfully, I have always been outgoing; hence the fact that I am writing a book admitting every mistake, failure, and moment of greatness I ever learned from. If I was doing this to cash in, I would write erotic novels. Have you read that stuff?! It's not only obtuse as a narrative, but this Fifty Shades phenomenon is horrifyingly perverse. Ick!

Recess for me was a gift from Odin. When we got whistled in from recess and I hadn't seen enough passes from our impromptu football game thrown in my direction I bordered on tears more times than I could remember. By third grade it merely motivated me to intercept more passes. This is why during and after school, physical activity is impossible to ignore. When I wasn't tossing a football or playing basketball, I was camping with the Cub Scouts. Street hockey was an institution in our neighborhood as children, albeit a dangerous one. Somehow we decided cross checking was legal in the grass. Nothing like a hockey stick to the chin to help you grow up, and these were the days of wood sticks before graphite. These are the types of games that will help alleviate malevolent or uncontrollable feelings they act on as a result of hyperactivity. ADHD collects into an entity sooner than

OCD does, and has more of a grip early on. When children are young they can be held down and controlled easily, but in fractured homes this vitriol can spiral into their teenage years. Pubescence can take control, and as they grow it can get worse. Usually this is more intrinsic with young bipolar and schizophrenic patients, but ADHD and Tourette's can make it crazy!

This is not meant to be a scare tactic. You are a reader I presumably do not know or haven't yet had the pleasure of meeting. I do not hold a crystal ball and cannot diagnose you with my history degree. I am one man writing from my life while trying to categorize yet not stereotype the experiences I've had as a youth advocate and later a mentor. I have helped some kids with some really nasty cases. While some could barely fit a word in, watching them struggle just to say something nice was as gut-wrenching as it was heartwarming.

Consider getting involved with other kids who have Tourette's. This does not mean that TS support groups have to be treated like a club and that everyone has to be friends. It just so happens that as I've matured, I've chosen to help others. My best friend all my life has Tourette's, but everything we've ever grown into and out of is because we have been on the same page. We have a mutual appreciation for Heavy

Metal music and the life that surrounds and is within it, while we also enjoy similar movies and cuisine. This isn't to say that the Tourette's didn't make us closer. I'm the talkative Type A while Alfred is the world's most stress-free person. It's awful that he lives in Oregon but life goes on, and you keep in touch. More reason to visit a place where the ultimate medication is legal, and experience the setting of Portlandia. TS became a shared experience, yes, but it wasn't ever paramount in the development of our friendship. In fact, if both our parents were not so actively involved in our well-being, we might not have ever even discussed it, and it is never part of our consistent whirring intellectual discourse.

What I'm getting at here is that friends don't become friends because of mutual medical conditions. We lean on one another, which I'm hoping this book encourages more parents and young people to do, but it isn't demanded that we become a big circle. Friends become friends because of mutual respect, similar tastes, and compatible personalities. I wouldn't purposely marry someone with Tourette's (Thor help this child!) so don't look for friends intentionally with TS, but always find a sturdy hand to light the way through tough times. This is true with anyone inside and outside the world of neurological medicine and support. These are lessons learned as a child, while using hindsight's perfect vision along with the input of my parents to understand their end of the story.

One thing I learned as a teacher (which is almost like an auxiliary parent who wishes they could spank your kid but cannot) is that treating a child even as young as six or seven as a dumbed-down subordinate screws with them and bites you back. Children need to understand that mommy, daddy, and teacher run the show, but that we do not look down upon them because they are young. Rather, we instill these lessons via respect and admiration, praising every victory while reprimanding defiance in a constructive way. I taught at a biblically oriented preschool and when I worked mornings, the old Southern Baptist ladies would come in to sing repetitive songs of Christian indoctrination. Every adult reading this book remembers that one old lady that scared them to death during preschool the way Commandants scared their victims during the Holocaust. It gets that bad. All you want to do is shrink away and disappear while they walk past. We had one particularly Jesus-crazed lady who I swear would lash the kids if she could. Harkening to the petulant fear I experienced at the hands of these same devil-kin in preacher's clothing, I would round my children up at 9:45AM, and speak to them: "Kids, you know who's gonna be here in 15 minutes. You're scared, I'm scared of her too, please do what she asks and we're going to get through this together." This is the way education should be. When my children acted up, I assured my authority, but when they were at their best, I was just another child scared to death of the Bible ladies. This is the same structure I hope will engender the educational system. My children knew I had their back, and they knew to protect mine with amicable and demure behavior. I loved them and they loved me.

Punishing someone with TS especially harshly can cause damages that wouldn't occur in otherwise "normal" children because their Tourette's makes them feel inadequate and self-conscious already. When they are aware of their conditions and believe that it is genuinely a reason to blame, this will hurt them considerably. However, some young punks might use it as an excuse to do what they want (exhibit A: South Park's Tourette's Special). I've never seen this before, but I've heard of it happening.

Tourette's is a very public disorder, in that it's easy to see and tough to watch. Like a derailing train or a shot of Jameson, it is hard to ignore and tough to digest. While many people are supportive there are some who just cannot help but put them down. If I gave by-the-book advice based on exactly how I lived my life, my message would be nothing but a litany of mistakes and failures written and woven within a grouping of successes. The key is to be honest and candid, with yourself and your family. There is no need to withhold anything, so use me as a model, and be open with your parents. The more they understand you, the more likely you will turn to them in times of need. My parents did well financially, which was a blessing, but more importantly, that through every crisis and throe of pain they were there to lend a hand. Yet as important as it is they be a rock to save a shipwrecked sailor, when seas are calm and the juggernaut that our life and vigor are crushing their way through a fleet of prior difficulties, you must be there in triumph as well. I was and still am a mama's boy, and my dad is as much a part of my being as my mother. They both have carried me through the agony and suffering of loss, while also celebrating every small victory hand in hand.

The more young people who with TS who use my message as an ancillary guide together with their parents the more I will know I have done something for all of you. Yes, I've written about sex, and bullies, and drugs, and hooch, but it's not narcotics anonymous in these pages, and they're certainly not testimonies and party stories. Every bit of this is a testament to the creativity in life, and failures and heights reached at any point. The nastier, admittedly more colorful chapters are there to show young people what they will undoubtedly face and exactly how to handle it once they have made a choice to take a step. One foot after the other, one rock after the last, we will climb the mountain together. As people, as afflicted, as conquerors.

SCHOOLS AND TEACHERS

If there is an area where not an ounce of objectivity or detachment will take place, it is here. This does not mean that struggling with the scholastic sphere will be everyone's problem. I had many amazing experiences in school and met some teachers and friends whom I've kept my entire life. I was not a true hellion in school, but my attention span combined with boredom created a deadly cocktail of needlessly obnoxious yet harmless behavior. Young people with Tourette's are not prone to violence. I've seen a lot more damage done by a kid raised by bad parents than a kid raised with Tourette's. Without trying to be too scathing, I will embark on a literary diatribe of sorts that I think will do society a lot of good!

I am likely more of a cynic than almost all Americans, so understand what I am trying to get across, but if the scholastic Russian Roulette is the game to play, those with TS must decide for themselves what he or she wants to do and experience in school. When I was entering pre-kindergarten at age four, I could barely tell the difference between my bed sheets and a urinal, so obviously I was stripped from the freedom of choice when I was entering my lifelong foray into the schooling world.

My parents were very hard workers, and were fortunate enough to have the fortitude and wherewithal to put me in a position to subsist in school. As a result, my parents knew there was some reason to place me in private school. I believe if they did not engender me early into quality educational institutions equipped partly to deal with me, my writing ability may have never manifested itself to the point where I could write a book. The class sizes were minuscule in comparison to public (or government schools, which I will elaborate on later) and individualized attention was possible. I was the only child in class that could read at an accelerated level, a trend which always followed me through the language arts. Every morning we wrote our plans through the "Class News." Dr. Haley (may she rest in peace, my long dead first teacher) wrote on a large flip book of note paper our schedule, the date, and a summary of adjectives to describe the impending beauty of our budding education. Some of the students asked such dumb questions that my four-year old self became a cynic.

I will say this multiple times throughout, boredom is Tourette's worst enemy. Pretty soon I fell in with a couple real goobers due to my lack of educational stimulation. We became known as the "three stooges" and consistently rabble-roused. We had to be separated in every class. This would be one of many times with which my schedule was altered to diffuse situations. This litany of skullduggery for my entire scholastic career was nothing but a blast to me. However, understandably, we really pissed off my teachers and professors. Education is no longer a way to raise a child, but a political process of indoctrination, that each day becomes more and more dangerous as we mask political correctness for kindness and forcible admissions based on ethnicity as inclusion. Merit is no longer the prime gradient in schools, it is based on a backwards set of Marxist ideals that begin at kindergarten and end at Muhammad. Don't believe me? Look into what some Common Core districts are bleaching the children's cerebellum with.

For most of my schooling, I avoided study groups and aced tests, while ignoring homework altogether . It was not because I was poor at homework (ok, I was) and it was by choice. Detaining me in a single sphere for six to eight hours a day, then spending three hours at football, one on the bus, and subsequently asking me to go home and accomplish more of their drivel was too much for me to handle. As a result, I have merely gotten by but never indicated my true intellect with my GPA. In college, with the temptations present, I became an even worse student. Furthering my disdain for education was the massive amounts of indoctrination that went on. We've heard much ado about Harvard students who believe America is more harmful than ISIS, with the same going on at Ivory Towers across the country. I would like to see them left in Syria in blue jeans and tank tops and see if they change their tune before they're burned alive for their "impieties."

What about the previously mentioned "government schools" diatribe which many surely are salivating to hear? I used to argue with my ex who was a National Honor Society member in a crappy part of Fort Myers. I always thought that government (or public) school education was so beyond inferior to global standards that my GPA was not an indicator as much as hers was. The bottom line is, this country has "standardized" everything with common core garbage, uniform IEP's that can be disastrous due to the uniqueness of Tourette's, and completely low standards which reinforce the stereotype that the United States is fat and dumb, while also pumping

East Asia full of pride. Furthering my assertion is the discrimination against Asian Americans in college admissions. Don't believe me? Look up the "bonus" system that Ivory Towers use to add points to SAT scores based on ethnicity. Asians actually are penalized. Yet, genetics have proven nothing about one group being smarter than the other, society and the familial structure have made the sliver of Asian Americans in our nation rise atop the median income categories and educational achievement. Couple that with the slimmest margin of single parent homes, and you have a recipe for success that the ethno-centric Ivy League has addressed with detriment. We've merely reversed segregation, and it has harmed our schools. No longer does the strongest and smartest reap the reward, it is now the melanin count that determines your eligibility for a high education. Colleges have become so ignominious with their discriminatory standards and political correctness that now Catholic colleges are even ostracizing students from classes for disagreeing with gay marriage. It is in understanding these bizarrely apologist policies in a place where, if any place at all, should be a haven for the free trade of ideas both pragmatic and radical, that forced me to not comply with the rules of engagement set by these laughable Marxists who descend from across the planet to distort American ideals.

This is a country that created the assembly line, the Bessemer Process, and peanut butter, and now we have kids who can't even read at an eighth grade level passing their senior year. School lunches are dreadful, and now taxpayers are on the hook for breakfast too, not to mention the complete lack of psychological and therapeutic services or recommendations. Some of these kids are powder kegs, ticking time bombs skulking the halls of government schools with absolutely no support network stemming from the school, but instant access to firearms at home. Birth rates have overburdened government schools, and more freebies are passed out to kids whose parents should never have taken the responsibility.

There are plenty of kids who do just fine in public school. Even some of us with Tourette's Syndrome do not have the luck or financial backing to survive in private school. I do not want to completely encourage or discourage any action by parenting readers. Yet, in my limited experiences in government school, my grades were non-existent because things were too trivial to bother with. I was under a veil of fear because kids were attacked for stepping on someone's new Jordan's.

So it is understandable that the boredom factor coupled with the instant availability of cheap drugs and frightening racial pressure not only put me on hold but made everything worse for me. My private schooling cost a small fortune, a fortune which I abused by completely neglecting many of my studies. If there is any way I could repay my parents for the waste of my education, it is to move forward with a starry graduate degree (unlikely) and move beyond the investment of education with career successes. I hope someday to repay my mom with a horse and stable, and perhaps a stocked wine lair for my father.

School can be a reasonable investment through the college years, but it is not always the best possible case. Thinking about it, the litanies within might make me look like a real ass, but never did my neglectful educational habits or any historical junctures in which I hit true valleys strike home long enough to disturb my life's trajectory. Better an ass than a liar anyway. A measure of success boils down to how readers learn to accept this as a treatise on life under this condition, and not a self-help "do this and not that" book. Let's be real here, I would have struggled significantly If I spent another minute in public school. The reason why IEP's (individualized education plans for students with extra needs) are sometimes ineffective for students with TS is not a universal sentiment for everyone. They really only address it with a blanket plan, and for people who are functioning there are few alternatives. Public schools do have programs for the disabled, such as those with Down Syndrome, but Tourette's cannot be placed in the same category. We are ubiquitously unique. In fact, if I combined every document I have typed thus far for this discourse, I may find one-hundred instances of that word: "unique."

Understandably, my criticism is scathing. I come from a household where we learned that rugged individualism and maximizing capable independence is a healthy alternative to free school lunch and a brain-dead education. Public schools are so crowded and so devoid of special attention that it can be a struggle for anyone. Focusing the education budget on inner-city vulnerable students is admirable, but becomes such a factor in the continuous fiscal maelstrom that those who are mentally and emotionally vulnerable are thrown by the wayside because of their gainful economic status.

I chose initially to try and ply my insight by teaching and coaching football. It would have been a blast, but soon I realized the danger of teaching. In public schools, unions are the norm. These unions drive up constantly avaricious budgets and demand for more and more money while public schools become worse and worse. The money doesn't go to education, but to monstrous union checks for their backed politicians.

It is not only political bias that lured me away from

even trying to apply at public schools. How about the fact that there are youth ganglands in many places, or that as previously stated the psychological services are so nonexistent that schools have become war zones? As much as the unions sucked in public schools, dealing with private school parents was nearly as daunting. These parents and their offspring feel as entitled as the broke parents expecting an EBT reload every week. They can be as challenging as any district board, poor parent, or student. The issue is the cycle of poverty is identical in nature to the cycle of wealth. Not from a fiscal perspective obviously, but from a human outlook. One side feels entitled because of whatever generational troubles they have had, and the fact that since the New Deal their families have been handed whatever they have needed to buy cheap food and milk. On the other hand, even if the parents made their own fortune and were not heirs or heiresses, their sense of elitism can be even more neglectful to reality and dreadful than the poor.

I was having a discussion recently with a really stupid girl who spent some time in jail with a contemporary. We talked about her friends, who this year have sadly dropped like flies. I asked her why she thinks so many fatal car accidents, drug overdoses, and alcoholic issues occur among her friends. Her answer was the same as why the poor become avaricious even with an absence of familial crime. They are handed everything and believe they are invincible. My parents have money, so I certainly was not raised by wolves. Yet, my parents would leave me to rot in jail if they had to spend ten dollars to bail me out. I never supercharged my car, got into coke, or sped for too long. The bottom line is I felt like I had a security blanket, but not a Kevlar vest. Nobody is bullet proof, so for one side to point to the other as the avidity-laden morons is erroneous.

I certainly never planned to make teaching a lifelong endeavor, but a decade of helping children with the type of insight I have from personal experience would never hurt. I am certainly not the Moses – the deliverer of youth with TS, but I have a big mouth that is too much a source of trouble not to twist into something productive.

The prose with which I have written this book thus far is about as professional as a four-o'clock bar conversation on a Sunday. What are we getting at by breaking our backs and brains to sound as fancy as possible? This is not a scholastic dissertation; it is merely a way to communicate with every one of you as if we were having this meaningful diatribe amongst each other as friends. By the time the true tribulations and temptations of any scholastic arena in any economic setting hit home, the preparation and homeostatic pulsations which drive our minds to succeed, fail, live, or die, will be second nature.

Parents created children, "gifted" with Tourette's Syndrome. We can wallow in our own slime like the entitled poor, or bathe in megalomania like the entitled rich. Finding a balance in life, hence the homeostasis reference, is the solution to parenthood, to childhood, to adulthood, to love, to marriage, and to education. The best possible parents were like mine, in my opinion. They were never afraid to release the fury of their fervor, yet knew when my heart was broken and I needed a shoulder more than a fist. My parents represented me in every which way, as my personal envoy, but never treated me like a king at birth. My parents never truly knew or understood what I was or what I am still capable of, but sometimes acknowledging anomalies and rolling with the punches is even better than forcing a plan down the gullet which is doomed for failure. Some things can never be prepared for, but luckily if a mutual respect is established at a young age, those with TS might still get thrown in detention for being a kid, but will never be expelled. My disciplinary record is a massive rap sheet of minor offenses. None of which were significant, none of which mustered the police or principals. I found a balance between acting-a-fool and maintaining a level of studiousness and extracurricular talent to keep me in between the clouds and the dirt. Isn't moderation part of life? Stay between peaks and valleys, not hammers and anvils, not frying pans and flames.

INTO THE FOG

Welcome to my dissonant tale of love and loss, of gain and growth. Though I encourage all to read this, I encourage my friends and readers, to not only actively read every page but engage others (and me if I have time!) in analyzing what's been read and how to use every folly and fortune to better grow in our cancerous society. Realistically speaking, there is 'R'-rated material throughout the book, but this is what sets it apart. It's super weird to walk into a therapist's office and talk about what impulses felt towards the opposite sex or what's been smoked or how much can be consumed at a party. However, it seems all discourse written about neurological disability is one of triumph and challenges overcome, and while inspirational, it is essentially a liberal utopian outlook of what truly is a mental dystopia – an eternal war between the governing bodies of the mind and social expectations. Now, honestly, as society makes pot less taboo, it never was this way for me. These are things that if we walk out of our agoraphobic bubble we'll stumble on. I'm not advising anyone to smoke dope or have as wild a time as I do sometimes, but there's certainly nothing wrong with reading about my experiences from an impartial point of view. If impartiality was more par the course, we might be talking about Casey Anthony and O.J. Simpson fondly as executions passed.

Alas, I've seen priests that are more accepting of my Black Metal and bong water than some atheists are about my attitude, so I can never believe in universal acceptance. Sordid individuals make their nests in all facets of society, despite the grounding in stereotypes. Universality is something that will never be achieved. Universal healthcare is a plan already failing in its infancy, social security is bankrupt, and the myopic dreams of a UN utopia in Europe has only crippled the system there. Whether it's policy or personality, one can never please them all. Nobody will never be universally accepted for who they are. There are all types – everyone from those kids that desperately believed they would grow to be the next Eminem in middle school who made fun of me for what I was to the professors falling over their own literature in love with themselves and so stubborn I can't even type my notes. There are a lot of lessons that these insolent children and boneheaded professors could learn "universally."

The only true consistency in life is that regardless of who we are as people, there will be ups and downs, dicks and pussies, and people who really will change our lives for the better, or set out to make it worse. When my poor little brother came home from college speaking of this Finnish professor who was a complete misandrist, laughing in his face instead of doing her job, getting him thrown from his dream school, I thought he was full of hot air. My brother is a bit more naïve than I was. Forcibly, I put myself in certain exigent circumstances that helped me grow a bit faster, even without maturing yet. He wasn't kidding, and this lady is literally the reason why there are people out there who find "feminists" to be completely mental. I guess writing this book since a breakup with the bitch of the millennia and now driven by vengeance by my poor passive brother sort of is a therapeutic experience. And while the passage of time will redirect our focus elsewhere from old news girlfriends and mongoloid feminists, it doesn't change the cataclysmic circumstances that at first gave birth to this letter to no one that became a book. I always loved writing, and when the keys flow, it's almost as if I'm creating my own musical symphony, but words are there instead of sounds. The atonal clacking of the keyboard is as much artwork as the Fur Elise, in my opinion. There are people who will try to destroy us, never back down. There are people who will heal us: always accept and appreciate them. Then there are people, positive and negative who will fuel us: fuel can be vengeance, it can be love, it can be hate, work, play, and anything imagined that motivates anybody can be used in a positive way. So as much and as easily as a jackass would huff and puff and beat up my ex's new boyfriend and ride out to break this feminist journalism professor down, we're going to write a book instead. Given the direction journalism has taken, now essentially the creators and arbiters between Obama and the unenlightened public, I bet she'll be rewarded for her gender bigotry.

I always thought I was too abnormal, abstract, walking the tightrope between genius and insane, to write anything and not have it viewed as some criminal manifesto by the federal government, who surprisingly, is bolstered by the same critics of the Patriot Act now caught in the act for text message seizures. I really hope none of the pics of my horn I sent to my ex or some sleeping ladies got taken! If so, read it and weep wretches!

See, there are several great attributes out there that

humanity largely calls their most desired. Loyalty, hard work, courtesy, kindness, humor, cleanliness, and a few other niceties as well. Beauty is in the eye of the beholder, my friends. I am a faithless, non-religious man, but one would find me castrating myself before I was caught cheating on a lover. I'll help an old lady across a perilous crossroad, but I'll honk the Hell out of someone that's driving like an idiot. I'm kind to those whom I deem deserving, but never waste my love on ingrates, and I'm clean as a whistle, but won't waste my time and resources on overworking. These are very LaVeyan principles, which have contributed greatly to a strengthened if not somewhat nihilistic future. I work hard, I dream big, and some out there might find this whole "I don't love people who don't deserve me" or the "I don't believe in the Bible" to be what they deem as "evil" or "incomplete." No human is complete. The closest thing we have to completeness anywhere is probably LeBron at basketball, but does that carry over to everything? Would he be so magnanimous if he wasn't making millions upon millions dunking on hapless centers? Who the Hell knows. Sometimes I feel like he takes too many jumpers too.

Humans are incomplete. I'm decent at drums, I'm alright at sports, I lift hard and run fast, I write decently, but likely my best attribute is my loyalty and charity to my friends and family. Previously I mentioned the outrageous lengths I would go to serve my family. I'm not bound in chains by my true creators (mommy and daddy) but I am selling my soul to my family, my pantheon, who bred me and fed me and made me into the closest thing to a man they could.

For every silly tale of marijuana and hooch, of sex and of violence, there is an equally important tale that is less metaphoric and cryptic. We will at the very least learn from what I screwed up, and how some notable experiences and thoughtful meanderings shaped my value system and how I implement it or withhold it in today's strange world. Nobody wants Tourette's, but as budding adults we have to take responsibility and learn from each other and understand that there is always someone out there who needs us as much as we need someone greater than us.

When I got dumped I was sitting at a sultry one-hundred-ninety-eight pounds. I ran into a dude with a Pantera shirt on who was in awesome shape. I saw he was younger, and what I could gain in fitness from him, he would get in life's experiences. Yes, I only have four and change years on him, but from age twenty to now I've experienced life at a frenetic pace.

In any case, Frank quickly became one of my best friends. We have so much in common, and we always go to Metal shows and jam out to some heavy business. There is nothing gay about a bromance, and nothing wrong with being gay. For those familiar with basic biology, let's discuss symbiosis. It is the relationship between two separate species who affect each other.

A commensalism type relationship is where one species benefits and the other is unaffected. This is the hardest form of symbiosis to assess. How about a whale and barnacles? Barnacles have a place to put their nasty suckers, and the whales just do whatever whales do. They make weird mooing sounds, swim in pods, migrate, and eat krill. Now parasitism is where a "parasite" damages a "host" and benefits from it in turn. Examples would be a fetus, a tapeworm, or my ex-fiancé whom I renamed to "Parasite." The government is another fond example, eating up all our accomplishments and spitting it into entitlement. Mutualism is where our lives become better as the result of a friend, and in turn they benefit from us. Frank is a prime example for me. I emerged out of my slate cocoon of depression and into a good friendship I've been lacking. Now I'm sexier than I was just days ago.

My mother always taught me to never even associate with someone who won't bring positive changes to life. It's not hard to do well and right, so show parasites no mercy. We'd all swat a mosquito, stake a vampire, and gun down a mugger, so don't let subtler parasites take away our livelihood and happiness. In short, move on and find more lichens to our white oaks, remora to our spotted eagle rays, Portias to your Ellens (did they break up?), left testicle to right testicle.

PROBABILITY

There are two certainties in life: death and taxes. There are few truer statements than that, unless you're on welfare. If you asked me where my life would be a week ago, I might have a completely different feeling about it. I have had very challenging weeks emotionally, but never let myself fall back down. With nobody to love me and no one to lift me up (save for family), failure is not an option. We've all done probabilities in school. If Jim has five blue marbles and three red, what are the odds he pulls out a red marble? See my point? Sticking to the marbles, if blue are the positive outcomes to a situation, the great marble scrotum of life, and reds are the negative, then you've become moderately successful at a three of eight clip of hurt and failure. What we need to do is optimize our life – all of it, to fill the bag with far more blue marbles instead of red. For example, what was the probability of marriage with my ex? Well, it decreased quite a bit when she broke up with me. However, there are peaks and valleys to every situation, and they are all in constant flux. If you asked me the probability of marriage to her when I was buying her an engagement ring, I'd shoot through the moon with bliss and say "two-hundred percent." Now, with all of the suffering I've endured, all of the emotional carnality and failure that she now faces daily, I'd reduce that to zero. The facts of life are constantly changing.

Inversely to all this sad, criminal hullabaloo is the probability of finding a lover to hold me by Halloween next year (last one turned out to be an epic evening). No one should ever put pressure on themselves to acquire validation. You simply can't rush like I have so many times before. That said, Halloween is an awesome holiday to have a lover and I'd prefer someone I'm well-acquainted with (the well-acquainted part didn't happen, but the lover part did). A mere four months ago I dreaded Christmas. Yes, the greatest day of the year, every year, even for whiny latte wielding atheists. Well, by the time Thanksgiving crossed I had reached a point where I could breathe again (literally, I was choking for weeks) and go out and get baked and dance with my friends.

And regardless of what further wounds were communicated by me from my ex I was better off in handling things. With a strong sense of self control, I maximized the probability of not devolving into some post-relationship psychosis.

The problem with me and a lot of dudes and gals with TS is we are the most logical, brilliant minds, but when we are asked to react to the forces of life, sometimes we really muddle things up. In our minds the probability of a tremendous outlook increases, but once we've been called to action, our logic goes out the window as impulsivity reigns true. The triad, especially ADHD, heavily affects the process of mobilizing a plan. We have to understand that both the spiritual and tangible in our hearts will be dramatically changed by our unique thought processes.

Until our minds mature along with our bodies to reach a level of self-control that gives us an opportunity to remove the edge of our personas, we will always be stigmatized. It took decades for me to actualize any semblance of self-control, but once I began to become aware, my rise to rationality was strikingly meteoric.

So yes, I did some soul searching. It's February 11, 2014, and I am still sad over everything that went down. Yet, if you got to know me after that all went down, you'd see a dead man walking. Yes, I am feral, and will always be a bit as such, but because of the shattering of my heart, I was able to mature at a rate of growth seen in dogs. Now, when having a conversation, instead of interrupting I calculate. In a dire situation, I assess and react accordingly. If someone talks to me, I always say the right thing. Intellectually and physically I've always been a man, but emotionally I believe that we with TS still belong to our childhoods. This does not make us impossible, but if the values imbued in us are violated, it is challenging for us to react accordingly. These skills are not acquired overnight, but being a socially integrated person is a great way to increase the probabilities of being able to implement the goodness in your heart.

There are some curses and scary machinations. However, incendiary warfare is never an option to absolve a breakup. I wouldn't be single in prison, if you know what I mean. My desire is to connect with people who have pained and twitched their way to the bottom. I am to be the sword and shield that lifts the broken from shadows and into the light of love and mirth, and the axe that cleaves detractors into nothingness. To do that, goals must be taken and broken down. Instead of setting massive goals, set small ones which can help you refine yourself into a path of greatness. This strategy is a human one, not one for only us.

For example, in authoring this book, I don't set a goal to finish the book. I set a goal to finish a chapter. Life is a chapter book, with great essays, poetry, prose, pictures, paintings, and pop-ups. I can only tackle one page at a time, so instead of dividing my resources and wherewithal to a gigantic loft, I climb each rung one by one – patiently, diligently, with valor and pride.

This goes for weight-loss goals as well. A goal to lose thirty pounds can instead be a goal to lose one to two pounds per week. This is the healthiest rate to lose weight, and by setting that goal in increments it becomes much more manageable. Add something such as a limit on fat and phasing out junk instead of quitting cold turkey (try eating more cold turkey). By training for patience, goals are rotating and revolving, just like probabilities. I set my goals high, broke them down, and chewed them up until I was happy with myself. I believe that if I cannot laugh at myself, believe in myself, understand that my emotions must be conveyed with logic, and have the patience required in such a setting of pending success, then I will always fail. As much as I'd love for this book to be done, I cannot write a shit draft or I will wind up not helping anyone. Paranoid by Black Sabbath was written as a filler song. Note its simplicity in structure and notation. This was a rare case of little effort and big result.

Nobody can become happy overnight, as I've come to know for most of my life's troubles. Times change, people change, and if goals and actions point in the right direction, good things will come from it. Weigh all decisions against the previous, observing oneself and the rate of maturity with which life is experienced. My maturity came forth in a hurry, but that's because the cataclysm which led to this book was like a quick poisoned dagger to the heart, and not a slow grinding. I told myself I had no choice, improve or die, because I wasn't going to live the way I felt and I wasn't ready for death. I made sure that everything I did was not a means to an end but a conscious effort to increase the potentiality of great things coming and the horrors of heartache leaving slowly but surely.

There are moments when survival and sustenance become a chore, but by still using what little charge I had to optimize my own life has paid off tenfold considering the position I could be in. Despite my confident appearance and my polished visage, the gentleman that girls who speak to is hiding a gaping pit where there once was a spirit.

I was patient. Instead of sleeping with every bimbo in Boca Raton and getting wasted regularly (there certainly was alcohol and Boca women though), I marginalized my recreation while continuing to use the feeling in my heart and the aching in my soul to learn what I had largely wrought upon myself.

One will reap what one will sew, life is a grand banner. Every day is a small stitch, finally leaving the sigil which is the crest of existence. That sigil and the integrity of every bob of the pin and needle depend all of us, and what we are able to do to protect ourselves from further harm in times of great vulnerability. I would rather have a dragon than a chicken as my sigil. If life, someone, something, unfortunate takes a poop in your room, don't carry it in your back pocket. Take that deuce outside and compost it, plant a banana tree, and watch the tree grow slowly, metaphorically denoting the stages of physical and emotional wellness. At some point, the choice you made with that shit that happened to you will provide a source of potassium, willpower, carbs, energy, and flavor, your totality in happiness. There may also be a few wasps nests. Plant a tree, don't stink up your bedroom. I know you can grow.

DRUGS AND ALCOHOL

From the moment I was out of diapers until the beginning of middle school, I was a serial bedwetter. It made sleepovers a fear of mine (despite luckily never pissing myself somewhere else) because being known as the fourth grade bedwetter is a social death sentence. It made me feel guilty, because to me it was my fault that my parents had to get up almost nightly at 3AM to strip the piss soaked clothes from my limp, lifeless body and wipe down my skin, now stinging from the ammonia. At one point they even bought a magnetized alarm that went berserk if it touched moisture. Even that couldn't deter Sir Piss-a-lot from destroying their nightly rest. I never spoke in detail about how despite the embarrassment and fear of word escaping the walls of my home, my greatest feeling was guilt. The guilt stemmed from waking my parents every night, sometimes even moving and taking a second leak in their bed. Then they became nighttime refugees, sleeping on the trundle bed - a twin sized rollout.

All of this was my fault, right? Well, recently delving into childhood memories, I realized that all of the piss drenched torture wrought upon my family for a dozen years was due to Haldol. Haldol is an antipsychotic, which like Risperdal is designed to treat symptoms of schizophrenia but carries over to slow tics. Now both have been mired in lawsuits, connecting the latter to gynecomastia, or swelling of breasts in men. I was a victim of poorly timed piss and man boobs for my entire childhood, and was even made fun of by my own brother for the nipples.

I have probably smoked upwards of a billion joints in my life and been so shamelessly drunk I couldn't stand, and never once did I piss all over my family under the influence of those supposedly deadly drugs. It's almost as if in our desperation to curb marijuana abuse (or enjoyment if you ask me) we forgot the real damage is done by Pharma. Allegorically speaking, doing this is like fighting gay marriage, when instead of focusing on halting organic love, we should instead work on repairing the American family, mostly in our urban areas. Despite the still vivid memories of pissing all over my family on an almost nightly basis, I feel more absolved now knowing that it was the mind numbing, genetalia destroying, breast swelling bullshit drugs I was on that caused the "golden" childhood I enjoyed each night. Fuck you Haldol and Risperdal. Any doctor who prescribes Haldol should lose his license. It is inhuman to put a five year old on a medication that, by the way, is used in median doses to instantaneously knock grown adult psych patients into an eighteen hour coma.

This section is probably going to piss off a lot of people. I wish more than anything that everyone – parents, students, priests, whoever – reads this with an open mind. How can I help if you don't know about me and everything that contributed to my failures and successes? Sadly, drugs and alcohol are just part of growing up. Kids and adults will be offered them, will see them, and may or may not use them. My mom is probably going to punch me several times in the face, because it would explain a lot. In order for people to clear their souls of whatever they deem as a personal mistake, they have to admit to those mistakes. Just like I admit that most of my relationship with my ex was my fault, I'm going to really quickly list all of the drugs I've used, and what type of reactions my unique mind has had to them.

This is not going to be a druggie library of reference, but we have to face it: drugs are real, and they are available everywhere. I've smoked marijuana, taken Xanax, obviously had a few beverages, taken LSD once, shroomed three times, molly, and that's about it. As a sufferer of TS, I highly recommend avoiding hallucinogens of moderate to severe effect. I did not enjoy my time on the magic mushrooms and would not dabble in anything created in a lab at this point. We all know that it's out there, and to circumvent the temptation we have to stare it down.

Let's first talk about the lab drugs. The FDA unfortunately has made drugs as medication so that I've been on the same cocktail of trileptal, welbutrin, and celexa (I eventually quit the celexa cold turkey due to its effect on my libido. Never quit a medication overnight. Take the advice). All of these drugs can cause significant repercussions such as seizures and heavy mood swings if I abstain at once. Thus, they have been a mainstay in my life by necessity. What can be more dangerous than a copious dosage of brain altering drugs? Perhaps these same drugs now ensconcing me in a lifetime of chemical dependency lest I seize and drown in my own saliva.

Well, unlike bimbos who don't look when a guy buys a drink for them, or some kid not knowing what he's into, I know. Thank the cosmos that nothing significant happened to me whilst experiencing these drugs. If I could give one piece of advice to someone who knows they are going to be taking drugs, it would be to avoid the lab created stuff. The approved and prescribed junk is harmful enough, but there are zero regulatory measures or supervisors when refining acid. Thus, you could have anything from a fake tab to a forever destructive experience landing you in prison, a hospital, or dead.

I really don't need to get into the nitty gritty of what these drugs "feel" like individually because this is not Jim Morrison's autobiography. Merely, I want to give my deeply honest opinion on the mistakes I've made and remind those of you on neurological medication that it can be equally as dangerous if taken incorrectly, in conjunction with other substances, or not taken at all. Unfortunately, dangerous recreation can be more perilous for us than the average person. Mankind is a completely varying beast, and nothing regarding Tourette's Syndrome can tie us together besides our diagnosis and our desire to succeed together. Everyone with TS has a different medicinal prognosis, prescription, and result. Drugs can be as dangerous as anything you do to yourself, a true at-your-own-risk assessment to learn about through experience. I can give advice as a seasoned young man, but I'm not going to stop or start anyone on any given linear path without their own choices made by themselves. It's like that time Reggie Miller scored all those points and New York blamed it on Spike Lee. As much as I can't stand Spike Lee, a taunting Afrocentrist film producer did not shoot the ball; Reggie did. If someone wants to destroy their life it's of their own volition, but I can tell you from my experience, as just that, not a suggestion, to the effects of marijuana and alcohol on my own life. We cannot absolve our sins until we've safely admitted to them.

I dated a total drunk, and it was a miserable experience. I was cleaning vomit constantly. With hooch and pot, you can moderate to an extent as is effective. A "functioning alcoholic" still has the term "alcoholic." Distancing them from their condition is like separating illegal from illegal immigration or Islam from ISIS. If you are unable to do these activities without successful moderation, you eventually become a complete loser. For whatever reason, when I have a few beverages, I go on autopilot. I always become a razor sharp flirt, and strangely always say the right thing despite my marginally unaware discourse. Much of it is understanding the playing field and my own limits, like finding that buzzed window where I'm unstoppable at beer pong. I can talk to someone in a state in which I will not drive and will make an extremely effective impact upon whom the discussion embraces. Sometimes, as is customary with liquor, my lips can get a bit loose and any shred of concern for the well-being of society is tossed out the window like an old fast food wrapper.

Do not litter, it is merely an epic simile. In any case, for example, some of the girls I've dated are completely mindless and stupid whilst drunk, and are incapable of making responsible decisions and incapable of learning from their mistakes. This is a commonality where my experience is an anomaly. We mustn't base our choice from anomalous ruminations.

The reason why I speak this way is not to boast of my somehow drunken skill, but it must be conveyed that being drunk and on drugs with TS is an entirely different experience. Drinking with fair preparation is also a wise move for anyone. Have a full stomach, drink slowly and nurse the beverage. I don't need to teach people how to drink, but when you face the liquor, know what its ramifications are. Know that many girls go from easy to a certainty while men just ask to be stabbed. Alcohol for me is liquid confidence, but for most its liquid stupidity. I also drink no more than once every few weeks. My commitment to rugby and my mental stability trumps my desire to let the liquor call the shots. With restriction I am able to responsibly care for my friends and myself, either offering a safe way home or accepting one if I cannot provide. Once someone gets to "that" point, you have to treat them like a toddler who needs a diaper change, and having changed diapers and taught Pre-K, I must say it is not attractive to be a drunk fool. I am physically active constantly, thus I am able to shrug off a hangover quite quickly. I don't know the identity, age, or sobriety of any of my readers, so I do not make any presumptions, but offer a fair warning that for the release of inhibitions alcohol grants, it can also bring disease, jail, or death.

Far less dangerous to my long term health in my opinion in comparison to the chemicals in my prescription drugs and the poison of alcohol is marijuana. Knowing the nature of it is intrinsic before taking the smoke or edible any which way. For me, a person of grandiose intensity and ferocity, marijuana takes me from a Bengal tiger to the Cheshire cat. Mostly, its calming effect is universal in its application to anybody. It can cause lung damage, heart rate acceleration, and extreme laziness, but the way I apply it to my life is different than most. I only smoke as a reward for a productive day. Instead of waking and baking, accomplishing nothing, I instead finish my duties – school, work, the gym, before I smoke. No, I'm not a NORML member and no I am not writing to you to suggest smoking pot, as its intended effect and makeup can cause issues with medication, as I previously mentioned. While I do believe its use for me is as effective, harmless and cathartic as anything

I've ever used, it also has another thing going for it: it is organic. When weighing the merits of legally bought alcohol and cigarettes ask these two questions: does this joint have arsenic in it? And how many people have gotten high and said: "I'm going to go kill people now?" Liquor has cost thousands of lives due to diluted sanity combining with the "come at me bro" machismo that men exude. Nobody gets baked and shoots up a school, just saying.

There are so many ways to die out there, that marijuana merely becomes a facet of life, and not a regarded danger. Furthermore, alcohol may be liquid confidence along with its poisonous idiocy leading to errs in life, but pot never caused a fight at a bar, would never cause as many accidents when compared to the number of drunk drivers, and certainly would take more than one stupid night out to kill you. If I had to choose one, I'd choose pot over alcohol any day, but I want more than anything for my readers to be as transparent and impartial as I am. You have to be honest with yourself, and depending on how many read that I'm an active smoker will decide how many times my mom lashes me.

No, but in all seriousness, folks need to prioritize the risks and rewards and mentally weigh them against each other. I'd be much more worried about my safety and the safety of others if I was drinking at the bar on a Saturday than smoking and watching a film at home. For many, pot slows them to a point of inaction, but youth obesity and underage drinking and cigarettes are far more a concern for action that the increasingly accepted cannabis. Society may finally wake up. Edgar Allan Poe was a drunk bastard, but am I going to pound gin while reading "The Pit and the Pendulum?" I think I've said enough. I cannot reiterate again that everything must be taken with a grain of salt before salting your cod, whilst being absolutely sure of the risks and possibly deadly scenarios that come along with drug abuse. I have my life together, and I'm certainly not a failure, but I do partake in smoking and drinking sometimes, I just know my limits and the powers that be, how they can destroy me, and how much it would take.

In order to protect yourself and your family from the dangers and risks of drugs and alcohol, one must research where the threats lie. And in an era saturated with political correctness and this socialist dogma of "fairness," maybe incendiary is what we need. Sun Tzu once said, "If you know your enemies and know yourself, you needn't fear the result of one-hundred battles." Drugs aren't your friend, but you need to assess the extent of the antagonism that drugs present to your life, and how extreme your falling would be if you lose your sense of restraint. Just don't be an idiot, and you'll probably survive a few mistakes. Don't wake up pregnant in a house you've never seen.

MONEY, AUTHORITY, GOVERNMENT, GOD, AND LIQUOR

I think it's an important PSA for the planet to discuss the relationship I've (and others like me have) had with capitalism, government, and God. I would say reluctantly that there are many others with various neurology abstractions that could echo these sentiments. A major component of these litanies of disability is the adamant rejection of authority, for me to an extent where I actively seek to break limits and laws. Now, despite the fact that I am openly declaring my want and desire to commit petty crime, someone with Tourette's will not always ride these compulsions to the extent where they commit thrill-kills or armed robberies. If an individual becomes homicidal or advantageous of a window to steal by strong-arm, it is because of their own criminal impulses, and not due to TS. And since most crime is fiscally motivated, I do not ever believe I'll venture past petty theft and planting weed, which is more of a convenience and a backstab than an actually profitable venture.

And since government and religion are the two greatest money vacuums on planet earth, and while their authority grows in its ubiquity, it is important to discuss the relationships these major entities have with one another. I was spurred to write this chapter when I parked my Honda in the street against the grain of traffic, and was then firmly instructed by my mother about it. "You're twenty-five years old and still don't realize you'll get a ticket!" To me, the direction of my car was inconsequential. Its arrangement in relations to my property was to me acceptable. It was on the grass, out of the way. For the cops to swoop in and ticket me for parking on my own lawn is something that my mind cannot fathom, but it happens all the time. You have to be either really dumb or drunk to hit a parked car, and what does it matter which way it is facing you? For an individual to wander onto the family lawn and tattoo my Iron Horse with a dirty, government, money-sucker receipt was enough for me of course to fire back with a sharp comment stating my disdain for their intrusion. Basic liberties, protection, and acquisition of property are necessities of freedom that our founding fathers fought hard to protect, only for an abomination of government beginning with FDR and his Social Security disaster (a true centurion of leftist failures metastasizing into the fiscal cancer it is today) to annihilate it and transmogrify such a hallowed discourse on nation building. To me, the ability to pettily steal and cheat from this diabolical theft agency is a rush. Sometimes I cannot tell if my Tourette's is me, or if these rampant and anti-authoritarian decisions are made as a result of a separate voice within me compelling such mischievous behavior; but it really doesn't matter as long as I am acting out the impulses which I feel led me to a better life, fulfilling my innate desire to strike authority down with even the most minuscule of offenses. I really thought during my jibber-jabber with mom that it was unimaginable for a cop to ticket me on my own lawn. Obviously I knew it could happen, and my mom was right, but perhaps that disconnect is a small example of how an entire country that thinks it is normal can't see eye to eye with people like me. This isn't a critique of cops. They get enough flak from the liberal media every time they shoot a blunt thief (we all know the Michael Brown situation was a politicized and unfortunate farce). That'd be a different book altogether. Cops are merely the vassals of an order of men and women who find it decent to charge $120 because a guy wants to park on his lawn facing – gasp – that way!

I do believe, given my political sentiments leaning towards Libertarianism, that the freedom of the individual and his earnings is the fundamental principle, and that under the Obama administration my sardonic behavior and tangential petty crime has risen due to its policies. Yes, the outside world can dramatically affect the way my disorders communicate with it. An example being, the President's executive power and his seizure of the freedoms within the private sector. It's hard to justify a president that ramrods blanket socialism via executive fiat as law, and then points to congress as if they're the derelicts, while by and large holding majorities for most of King Hussein's reign. As the federal government begins its wretched apotheosis towards a Godlike umbrella, covering the entirety of the entrepreneurial US citizen in its shit blizzard power grab, I find myself continuously deviating from the normal standards of the law.

Since I have grown more distant from our federal system and its pathetic half-citizens I pay for, I have bought a marijuana plant and stolen as many small items as discretion would make possible. It is suffice to say, that this is the very limit with which I will place myself into, as larceny and person to person crime are best left to the true criminal. The idea is not the fascination with liquor and weed, or even the necessity to make additional income. Merely, it is a way of promoting a usurpation of as many petty laws as possible. And, while these are indeed crimes, the difference between myself and a true criminal is that I feed on the compulsion to fight against a system that is taxing the shit out of me and making war upon my coffers, whereas the criminal does it uncontrollably, in the case of severe crimes purported by the unfortunately mentally ill, or out of necessity such as turning to crime to provide for the family whereas gainful employment was not viable to the criminal.

I've always tried to push the buttons of society, ask questions that make it uncomfortable, press what I can and cut my losses. This is just my way, and I believe it is the way of many with the authority complex I possess, but also with the mental and intellectual wherewithal to never take it to a level that would truly harm someone or themselves. I believe that's where the line is drawn, not between myself and the law, but between Tourette's Syndrome and more severe, less fortunate mental disabilities that cause delusions of grandeur, inner voices, and personality deviation. And while it is truly a depressing issue that the United States clearly hasn't properly addressed, given its multitude of law students and lack thereof in med schools, it is also a dubious specter with which I never face. And why would anyone want to be a doctor when their own government goes above and beyond to destroy them while creating and maintaining laws that line the pockets of personal injury lawyers?

I also feel that ODD, or Oppositional Defiant Disorder, is a farcical disorder created to justify children's authority complexes. Much like in the 90s, it seemed every boy between the ages of four and twelve was diagnosed with ADD and pumped with Ritalin, despite the proliferation of their diets with soda and processed foods possibly contributing to their hyperactivity never viewed as an option by idiots who spend a decade in school and are paid six figures to come to the realization of what I just outlined for you in a half paragraph. Kids would come to lunch in first grade with Fruit by the Foot, Pixie Sticks, Fun Size Hershey's Milk Chocolate, Capri Sun, Goldfish and a tuna sandwich of half mayonnaise and we'd diagnose them with phantom disorders and drug them before simply reassessing the sixty-five grams of sugar we're putting in a kid that barely weighs sixty pounds. ODD, I feel, while the scientific community views it as a true disorder, is total bullshit.

While I believe an element of the way I rationalize my worldview is a result of Tourette's and whatnot, I also feel that the easiest way to solve a problem is create a new one. Meaning, if a kid is hyperactive, instead of investigating his diet, his home life, or the amount of activity he's getting outside, drug him and slap a brand on him. ADD has almost become a franchise, and drug companies have made gazillions off of Ritalin, Adderall and others, not to mention the creation of the college student's (and Seattle Seahawks') favorite pick-me-up. Many of these ADD medications now are street sold commodities, in the same vein that we now receive forty hydrocodone pills because we're too feeble to deal with our wisdom teeth being pulled. How about the fact that when I was growing up I got hours of playtime outside but was still uncontrollably hyper. Now we have kids fed common core education that converts their brain into a leftist fed, milled robotic element. Instead of a mind, the government wants a hard drive, one that never asks the hard questions or dissents. Their recess, fine arts, and periphery education is stripped and they're left with this nonsensical formulaic work destined to turn their minds into an assembly line, one full of forced rhetoric and glorification of Islam. Then you take them out of school, where at lunch they've been loaded with terribly unhealthy foods (unless of course Michelle Obama has her way with your district, and then they starve) and they come home and jump right in front of the television. There's your ADD, and why every generation since my grandfather's has become more reliant and dependent since.

My mom despises the fact that I have a marijuana plant, or that I plunder my college campus of small household goods, or that I plan on making liquor. I can't possibly ask such a principled, majestic human being to ever understand the rejection of authority that presses me to these acts of seemingly stupid risks taken for little to no gain. It does in fact upset me that my mother disagrees with my lifestyle, but she possesses the normalcy which differentiates me and others like me from the remainder of civil society. That is compliance, of course.

Individuals within the autism spectrum, such as myself, are capable of placing each minute task and decision into such a fragmented, fractured lens that it is difficult to do anything without questioning, re-questioning, trying, retrying, and finally drawing a conclusion, only to second and third guess it. It's as if even taking a piss is approached with the scientific method. Such is life for us, and this is why our minds are constantly whirring, and why my mother is sound asleep in this New York City Hilton while I am pecking away mightily at my keyboard in an effort to explain to the world why things are how they are for us.

I believe that many humans metaphorically see the world through binoculars, with such stunning focused clarity, it's easy to approach and breach a single problem and solve it. People with Tourette's see things through a kaleidoscope. Because of the incredible assault on our worldview by Tourette's Syndrome and her sassy sisters, we have greater issue tackling a day-to-day task or problem, but often the solution is creative and is approached from a variety of angles. This is why many of the more famous individuals with Tourette's Syndrome have been artists or performers, such as Mozart, for example. Often the effort is more daunting, but the result becomes more breathtaking.

It's also why our creativity, such as the book you're reading, is normally expressed in massive machine-gun like bursts instead of a progressive, workmanlike authorship. Every writer is different, but for me, the creative process is one of immediate inspiration and action. Outlines, plans, dictation, and invention are not the strong points of individuals such as myself. We instead defer to the light bulb above us and explode onto the scene. We can reinvent the wheel and make it faster, but don't ask us to build one.

While my tics have dramatically improved over the past decade, the personality complex has only worsened as my intellect has sharpened and my viewpoints have grown more cynical. It's hard for me to walk down a street and not react to the stupidity I see everywhere I go. For many people, minor problems are swept under the rug, but when you see the world through that kaleidoscope, every detail, shade, color, hue, and issue are illuminated and distributed into their own brain compartment. Since the endless hard drive of my mind has yet to be silenced, my mouth, pen, and drive to cripple the authoritarian government and religious industrial complex which has saddled the world in fear and paranoia are still aflame.

This book began as a reaction to an emotional cataclysm following a destructive breakup, and subsequently evolved into an acerbic social assault that attempts to deconstruct as much as I've come across in this past year. It certainly doesn't help that I have my apartment to myself, and lack the oft aforementioned consistency of a regular lover, or even a dog or roommate. This is my life, and as I've sat forlorn penning this book, it has helped me grow as a man and a writer, imbuing me with the social commentary and self-dissection that I hope will open the window into my soul.

We live in a society today where the saying, "The truth hurts," is taken so beyond seriously that we now find it insensitive to say or do anything despite its truthfulness, and even its necessity to be said. Pervasive political correctness has created a dissimulation against free speech and truthfulness that I plan to use my career to destroy. Whether it is a compulsion related to my Tourette's Syndrome or merely a desire to see society grow back its standards. Disagreeing with the current norm is now consistently some form of bigotry, as the government continues revving the blades of its silencing machine. While this book itself covers many topics within the realms of neurology and psychology, I plan on utilizing this career to obliterate unnecessary sensitivity, wasted apologies, white lies, and totalitarian overreach. I want those who would abuse our nation's tenets to shudder when they read what I write, and to fear the next word to leave my lips. As Western society continues to, for example, protest for the immediate release of cop killer Mumia Abu Jamal but vilify Donald Sterling, possibly suffering from dementia in the first place, its double standards and nonsensical sensitivities run amok. This isn't to say that what Mr. Sterling said to his (possibly?) prostitute girlfriend is acceptable by any stretch of the imagination, but as a free-spirited young professional, I am under siege. It's easy to see that as the government and religion continues its accelerating invasion into our daily lives, raiding our paychecks and limiting our freedoms humanity has caught ablaze.

It's almost reminiscent of the simplicity of the 1920s, even with the depression. The Twenties had no Hitlers or FDRs, no Stalins or Mussolinis and consequently, no global genocides. Unfortunately, this has become mirrored by the drastic differences between the 90s I grew up through, and today's shit storm. Granted, the entirety of the 20th Century could be known by its shameful inhumanity. And while we can chalk up the past to ignorance or blind faith in a vengeful God, the 20th Century was one of supposed progress. The Herero Genocide of 1904, the Armenian, Rwandan, the Holocaust, Rape of Nanking and others came to characterize such a bloodbath of a century. Yet, in my lifetime, I have watched the government continue to grow along with the emboldened Islamists and freeloaders on welfare we have today, resulting in the most grandiose barbarism to occur in my lifetime. What's bewildering to me is that private citizens continue sipping their frothed milk and listening to Dave Matthews Band while repeatedly voting for politicians who tout increased government influence to remedy the world, whereas we all know the more power government has the more people die. The hypocrites are eternal. "Keep your government out of my vagina!" they say, when they're ready to abort yet in the same sentence want me to subsidize their birth control. As governments grow and freedoms are restricted, so does the opportunity for radical imposition. Yes, this book was supposed to be mostly about Tourette's Syndrome, so maybe I dropped the ball on that one. Perhaps this in itself is microcosmic of the cranial hullabaloo that occurs in each passing thought.

Watching this capricious malediction characterize parts of this book, for some, will be a deviation from what the core message is, and it will surely achieve a thorough lambasting by the New York Times, who in itself has about as much journalistic integrity as Hitler's personal PR firm, but that's beside the point. I believe that these meanderings are, in fact, a piece of the puzzle. It shows the reader just how quickly someone with my complexities can deviate from the norm, and in its own way provides two layers of commentary. The first being the obvious and near-criminal sentiments I have and others like me possess regarding authority and the extradition of freedoms, whereas the under-city of this construct displays the whimsical means in which someone within the autism complex thinks. In that way, this could be academic. It skirts the line between someone truly deleterious writing a memoir from their days as a criminal, and an academic writing about the nature of a disorder they do not possess but have studied intensely. I believe many like me have enough self-control to maintain their standing with society, but lack enough to truly fall within the herd. The black sheep, if you will, is what I am. I'm still a member of the flock, but I will never follow the shepherd. By societal deconstruction, I do not speak like a Tyler Durden, simply sewing chaos for the sake of it.

In any case, I am not an anarchic individual, but I foresee a simpler world in which government and God's inclusion in my life is ancillary and predominantly by choice. Given the fact that both demand my money to feed the destitute who refuse to work, it is easy to see why someone such as myself desires its ultimate degradation. Government's presence is, to an extent, necessary, but it has exploded into this soft dictatorship that is just perilously exploiting its constituents and violating the bill of rights it was sworn to uphold. Use my taxes to fix potholes and help veterans, not 30k a plate fundraisers. My young adulthood could be defined by dissention, but rarely in history has an individual ever changed the world without smashing the idols of falsehood and shattering the shackles of mental and physical slavery. Moses freed the Jews at great cost, Washington established America amid a necessary bloodbath. Hitler was taken down in a combination of his own arrogance, American and British tactics, and Soviet aggression. Rome rose and fell due to several outstanding warlords on either side (among many other factors). Such is the rule of nature, in which the strongest shall survive. Our borders have been forged in blood and torn down by a government which will oversee the greatest bloodbath in this young century thus far. What is known is that each time the world has changed for better or worse, it has had two consistencies: a primary instigator, and red rivers of blood. While I do not wish to serve as this primary sparkplug, it's easy to see why someone bearing the marks of my disorder would. Oft times the most successful CEOs, commanders, and even performers of the world have had some neurological component that never degraded their intellect, but slanted their train of thought. For me, the world beaters, nation builders, and nation destroyers all saw through a kaleidoscope that one could never pursue with their black and white binoculars. While seeing through that metaphorical kaleidoscope is challenging and sometimes even refreshing, it is a persistent fight to see eye to eye with anyone through that lens. Not every thought is destructive; as many great legends of business and invention (Howard Hughes anybody?) were spurred by their obsessions, but the potential is there for a myriad of options taken from a simple spark, thought, or ideal. Because of these built in complications, I chose to write chapters about substance abuse, relationships, and other machinations that in my life have created and destroyed so many friendships, ideas, and lovers. Tourette's Syndrome has permanently impacted my worldview, and it could have me in a penthouse or the big house, on death row or the winner's circle.

Only time will tell what the product of my lifestyle and its pairing with my disorder will create in the coming years.

As Joshua tore down the walls of Jericho, and as Joan broke the siege of Orleans, I am on my own quest to do as much as I possibly can to revert the world to its prosperous standards and immolate the tide of stupidity that has perverted my generation.

ON DETESTABLE PEOPLE

I get along really well with my stepmother. She's as kind and caring as any non-blood relative could be and all her hard work culminated into a successful career spawned from cold litigious facts. She and my father have risen to the apex of their practices, and for that I am proud. So when the time came for my parents to divorce, and for them to both nearly immediately supplant one another with live-in relationships, albeit my father spending a bit of time at his bachelor apartment first, I was ready. I was quite taken aback by the news, convinced that the reason my brother and I were solemnly called to the table that scorching July midmorning of 2007 was to announce that finally my beloved Nanny, Rhoda Siano had passed.

Well, as though I was sideswiped by a different

form of family division, my relief was still palpable even though I showed compassion and disappointment in and to all the parties involved. I thought my parents were inseparable. It was exceedingly difficult to fathom that my father would be gone by the early afternoon, his bags covertly packed and the divorce announcement mercifully postponed until I had enjoyed the frivolities of prom and graduation in a white collar private school. Despite my immaturity ruing the day in 2007, I, unlike every 90s movie stepson, gave Amy every possible chance to prove herself worthy of the father whom I spent my life idolizing. The majority of circumstances behind the divorce were acrimonious as far as my knowledge is known, and I didn't dig for truth during such a mess. Amy proved herself wholeheartedly to be a good candidate for my father's second wife. Howard, similarly on my mother's side, has been everything I had hoped he would be. The result, after years of bitterness, are two separate former lovers in two very happy relationships, all each a part of my life on a daily basis. I can't imagine a more successful divorce. Yet, of course the ebbs and flows of emotion and scorn were always there. In no way is my relationship of two years and change with my ex comparable to a thirty-year romance that ended in two kids, two homes, new families and alimony fights, but in seeing my parents successfully move on after so much they shared and split over, I knew it was in me to stop being such a sissy.

That said, for the longest time I was afraid at annual birthday gatherings that my mom was going to produce her Beretta and open fire. Then, I hearkened back to one of the most invaluable lessons my mom ever taught me. My mom has no reason to like my father or Amy, and just like my ex thought I owed her common decency and to let her crawl her filth back onto my radar, such a fairness does not exist in love and war. I gave Amy every possible opportunity, as I said before, to do right by me, and she passed with flying colors. Obviously, this test does not apply to my mother's relationship or lack thereof, and whether or not she actually is still pissed over it is something I do not know and highly doubt. At one point my mother, rightfully so, was angry and when she asked me how I dealt with a new family I was unfamiliar with, I told my mom that everyone has to deal with things or people they are unsure of or completely despise. I never went through a moment in my life where I was unsure of Amy and my father belonging together, as they are peas in a pod, perfect for one another, but there are moments each day outside of this solitary example of dealing with people that in some sort of significance or lack thereof get into us, under our skin, that try to rend our flesh and maim our hearts, and they must be destroyed.

Obviously, in today's "Everybody gets a trophy, non-duelist, post-feudal" atmosphere, we can't simply hone our combat skills and slay people we don't like. If that were the case, as permitted by law, I would have a scroll stapled to the wall of all the dicks I slayed that hung around my ex like the homeless around a garbage fire when I was still pissed at her and all that nonsense. In fact, there are so many candidates and applicable situations where sabre waving would be the most pleasant and easiest way to finalize a dispute. However, thanks to the callousness of Aaron Burr, Andrew Jackson, and the modernization of humanitarian standards, we are no longer able to simply destroy those who detest us or cause us to detest them. For those with TS, from the very onset of first twitches, they are going to encounter people who are unsure or merely despise them because they cannot help what they are. In many ways, the words and hurtful names I was called so often as a young child still hurt. I'd been struggling to understand my affliction then, and in today's society those words and hurtful names would be regarded as bullying along the lines of discriminating against the mentally inept or simply strange, like myself. Making fun of someone because they twitch or blink their eyes is no different than making fun of someone because they are a different color. The only difference is the lack of high powered liberal attorneys and community activists representing the Tourette's bunch. Thankfully, because growing up with such a public and noticeable disability is hard to live with, often aesthetically more than anything, the TSA has spent considerable portions of its disposable resources in funding programs and educational materials to nip these offenders in the bud.

Such was the case as my transfer to North Broward Prep in the seventh grade. I was encountering stuck up rich kids whose parents would buy them a German coupe for their sixteenth birthday (it's no wonder why so many kids from the Coral Springs to Boca area die of overdoses and car wrecks) who would without a doubt pounce upon me at the first opportunity to ridicule as if they suffered from some kind of egotistical vampirism that was only fed on the tears of other children. Those assholes! And I knew that even though I wanted to pick up a desk and throw it at them, society would not accept such barbarism, and I would lose my place in a program specifically designed for the illiterate, the incredibly-attractive-but-not-very-smart, and the hyper and twitchy. I fell into the latter, and unfortunately our very worst readers were given parts in English class like Macbeth in Macbeth or Othello in Othello. Nice.

So, in my early few weeks of a new school, I was able to somehow, surely with a lot of pushing from my parents, corral the entire grade to explain the condition I have. The finality of the event was the complete approval from everyone in the room and the lauding for the courage of such an endeavor. Despite standing there in a room full of new faces and twitching in front of everyone, one year removed from the darkest year of my suffering, I was able to make friends with all on my way to a long and enjoyable middle and high school career. I was in the Jazz bands, on the football team, and won the Homecoming King, which was a great memory because my Queen Irene (yes, it rhymes) was and is literally the nicest girl on the planet. I hope she reads this and contacts me so I can feed her Panera and give her a hug. I had no qualms, after the initial courageous foray into a new school with new people, to dance the evening away with her and my friends. It is possible that this early burst of gregariousness surmised in the acceptance that I would universally enjoy at North Broward Prep. I'm not trying to reveal this history of my family as a dude writing a memoir, nor am I trying to pat myself on the back for showing this courage at thirteen, but I am speaking to reveal to you that anything is possible if you just do it. There are so many assholes and bullies out there that are searching for acceptance themselves, and if you give the world an opportunity to see you and how special you are, they will without a doubt give their hearts to you. People go into many events and new things with blank slates and unimportant circumstances, and to sway them a certain way with impressions, explanations, and the bravery to encounter society, know that if you are not open people will close themselves to you.

Let's be honest, everyone wants to know why a person with Tourette's can't stop extending their arms. They are all wondering, much like how everyone wants to know how the dude with one arm lost his arm, and that tension in the air is nothing more than human curiosity combined with your own peculiarities. These are the same reasons why Jane Goodall hung out with gorillas, or why Charles Darwin took the HMS Beagle to discover his origin of species. It's the same reason Christopher Columbus sailed to the new world, and it's also why wars have been fought, villages razed, and nations set aflame. It's curiosity. Sometimes the curiosity is lined in morbidity, or wonder, or potential gain, but if it's not sated then there will never be a solution to the divide between the curious and the curio. So I implore those with Tourette's, that in entering a conversation, if you see that tension rising, that need to know, explain to them that you're twitching because you have Tourette's

Syndrome. It's awful to say this, but I would not be surprised if certain women have been initially captivated by me because of my condition, as it's much like my nipple piercing and tattoo of the Witch King, forming a triumvirate of bodily talking points.

Treat TS like that fancy vase your mom goes on about, or the first edition books your local antique store has on display. If you have TS, other people will notice, and they have to know or they can be difficult to get along with. It is my hope that my unequivocal extroversions will do some of the legwork for you. I hope to God that more people without TS read this than do, because for everyone that finds some shred of wonder in my diction, they will already be approached with the understanding that the TSA has sought for decades. This book should hopefully, if it serves its intention, give us, or those of us with TS, the courage to know that someone else is out there and to get off of your tail and open yourself to the world, and bring to the prospective bully, girlfriend, friend, or boss a greater understanding that things are more complex around here than they thought.

You know those memes that go around about bullies like: "See that girl you called fat? She's got a glandular problem. See that kid you called ugly? He has a cleft palate." Apologies if I made light of those otherwise macabre and depressing bully awareness Instagram posts, but these are made to highlight that we just don't know shit about each other unless we find out from the source. If you asked my ex or her friends, they'd tell you I'm a devil worshipping maniac who revels in the sufferings of innocent babies, but obviously that would be a laughable lie, or at least an exaggeration of how I really feel (joking!). If you asked my mom, she would tell you I'm a whirling dervish of energy and passion who is struggling to find his way but is getting there. If you asked any of my friends, they'd probably tell you I'm a nice guy. You just don't know, and unless people understand you and what your story is, you can expect them to treat you like shit. Most of the time people are naturally repulsed by what they don't understand, to the point of fear.

This is the reason why the fear of God inspires religion, and why the fear of religion inspires atheism. It's why American Indians who dressed in cloths and used antiquated weapons against the industriousness of Europeans and their encompassing God were seen as savages. It's why they were destroyed. Misunderstanding, or the outright refusal of mutual appreciation, is why people are dicks to each other. To me there are three kinds of person-to-person interactions: one where you are an unknown, one where you have an opinion rendered based on your interactions with the subject, and one where regardless of your interaction the other party will have rendered an opinion. The first is how most friendships, marriages, and partnerships are built. With the advent of the Internet dating age, fewer of these variables are in play, which in a way is nice as you already know what you're seeing before you lace up your dancing shoes, but it also takes away some of the mystique in dating. The second is one where your actions have deserved in one way or another, an opinion that is rationally based upon the most recent or a string of associated actions. This is the relationship in which you have earned a verdict. These are usually the relationships that have an endgame. Whether it's a compatible friendship, business, marriage, or divorce, these interactions are neither vitriolic nor positive, but are based individually upon the conversations and events in which the two have taken part. The third is of the virulent type, in which someone either doesn't or does like you for absolutely no valid reason. Some irrational bullies fall into this caste, as do those who fell in love with Obama because he was black, or refused to vote for him only because he was. It also is the reason why cockneyed smack addled, brillo-pad-headed idiots like Russell Brand have legions of stupid people willing to lick his crotch for recognition. Never try to sustain a relationship based upon this third premise. That's sort of why I have no care in the world as to who my readership becomes, as long as everyone is genuine and appreciate, positively or not, what I've written because of the message and not because I become some fashionable, trendy young author.

Although that pipe dream would be a great life to live, I would rather be adored because of the man behind the book, not because of the book itself or any successes that are a result of this production. Kim Kardashian is a perfect example of an entire legion of lovers and fans as a result of this third premise. She was a small time model, as far as I know, who didn't become anything until she had sex with that black guy on tape. Not only was the production poor, but I've never heard of the other supposed celebrity penetrating her either. So when I saw this, and watched her fame blossom as a result of her foray into sex tapes, I understood that it doesn't take much to be famous and to be famous is to have millions base their opinions on some sort of aesthetic exposure. That's why I thought that after so many years of playing music and watching actors and all that, if I were to ever become famous it would be with the written word.

There's no charade like there would be if I were covered in corpse paint and steel spikes playing blast beats, nor as a paid liar like an actor, whose entire life is based upon portraying the lives of characters more significant than their real selves. With writing, I can write whatever I want and can deliver a message that can be as watered down, as cryptic, as open, or as bat shit insane as I want it to be. I can choose the avenues of production and weed out any who would wish to silence me in lieu of increased publishing revenues. I can shut down this whole thing at any time if it goes sour, and nobody will pressure me again. The finest part of this entire publishing career that hopefully starts between these covers is that I have a group around me that doesn't want to doctor what I say to sugarcoat things. To do so would be to undermine the entire aim of my career.

As a result, the more extreme I've become over the years, the more loved or vilified I am. I can't stand people with mixed feelings about me. I either want to be loved, or hated, and no matter what I want to be relevant, because my message will help so many, of this I am confident. People with mixed feelings about me are like independent voters, or people who registered to vote only for Obama but had lived through four election cycles. They're the dumbest, most easily swayed hapless schmucks on the planet. I know my mom is an independent voter, and realistically I'm only registered to one political party so I can have a vote in the primaries (ask Thad Cochran if that even matters anymore), but to be unsure of oneself leading up to an election cycle is like living three of four years with no purpose or principle only to be wooed by a few snarky debate comments and promises of cell phones and food stamps. So apologies in advance to all you independent voters out there, but you shouldn't really even be making a choice if you have to wait all your lives to make it. So, rant aside, yes I want to be either loved or hated. For an individual to have a strong opinion about me either way is for them to state that they have a value system that is either aligned or contradictory to mine, and for that I can admire and thank them for merely reading, learning, and rendering an opinion. People that love or hate me are the folks who deserve to have a strong opinion in the first place, and all their interactions fall within that second category, beginning as the first, an unknown, and ending as either friend or foe in the third.

This is not to say that a fleeting opinion of anything is not normal. I only eat olive tapenade if I'm really, really hungry. When I'm famished it's delicious, but given a choice I will avoid such a concoction. Yet when it comes to things as monumental as politics, religion, and the colleagues around you, the only opinion to have is a strong one. So it is safe to presume that if I were to write a political book the Obamazombies would hate me whilst the Conservatives in hiding from the NSA-IRS-EPA-ATF Gestapo conglomerate would laud me. That's the way things should be. Division is inevitable in everything we do. It's evidenced at the election booth, at any bit of news, in music, films, and any other choice-based option grounded in personality.

Since duels and trials by combat are no longer means with which to seek redemption or settle a score, we have a passive-aggressive society who uses the Facebook rumor mill as its finest weapon. As a result, we have a mistrusting group of millennials that will sleep with one another at the drop of a hat but will never respect each other. Sometimes, the way we deal with detractors and detestable people in our lives will reflect on how others feel about us. Anybody can load a shotgun and kill people, but constructively dealing with upsetting situations and the people behind them is one of the defining hallmarks of a successful person. Countless volumes of timeless books such as Robert's Rules of Order, The Games People Play, and The Darwin Awards are written about conflict resolution. Since we no longer exist in a medieval society where village raids are the means to solve a dispute, we have to collectively gather ourselves and attack a situation with cleverness in lieu of violence.

My ex for the longest time thought I wanted to kill her. Why would anyone as logical and reflective as me waste my life behind bars when I could instead watch her run her life and her relationships into the ground from afar? It's really easy to ruin your life, and not everybody needs a helping hand. It can take thirty years to get where you want to be, and one racist email to tear it all down in seconds. Yet, apparently my dirty looks and semi-solidified muscles were enough to inspire fear, for whatever reason. The Teddy Bear Tony that everybody knows I guess to her was the Terminator, or a Kodiak Bear that hasn't been laid in six months. Suffice to say, I am not permitted to go to that gym for another year. It was a gym I loved, with people I loved, and an environment I was familiar with. And like most things I've screwed up or been screwed over for, I guess my dirty looks were too convincing. So when I was told that I couldn't return to the gym for a year, I respectfully acknowledged and ran with the fallout despite my disagreement with the decision. Anybody can be pissed off and do something drastic, something emotional. But a true warrior is patient, and focuses more upon refining his own skill and character than that of his foes. Knowing the situation, who was at hand, and my own self-control led me to take such a slight in stride and move along at the same breakneck clip I have been for the past eleven months.

Most of the time people do something stupid

they're relying on their emotions for consultation. That's how terms like "passion kill" "thrill kill" "crimes of passion" and "fatal attraction" are born. There's a common line in dumb decisions, and that's us checking our brains and our human instinct at the door to only follow our heart. And despite how many clichés there are about "following your heart," you really can go wrong in a million ways. Bad relationships are born from emotional vulnerability and bad decisions are made from the same sentiments. It's hard to say whether or not I would characterize Tourette's as an emotional disorder, but I do believe there is a reliable certainty in my own self study of OCD that sometimes our mental governance is dominated by our emotions. Sometimes people make some really bad decisions against their greater logic, and as of late my decision making skills have become Vulcan-like in nature. Now, this is not to say that my increased reliance on logic has removed all elements of human error or emotional connection to the world. I merely am smart enough now to know that to rely on emotion is to bring myself into a sphere of madness, in which the innermost sanctums of my feelings house my cerebral strategies.

It seems as if we have two personalities, one in which approaches our best interests with logic and one that approaches our interests with heart. Almost

Jekyll and Hyde like in their appearances, my improved persona and increased critical thought in approaching everything in life has led me to the inquisitiveness of Jekyll while simultaneously quelling the addiction that Hyde presents. In the story by Stevenson, Jekyll's addling results from his near addiction to the fearsome and powerful Hyde. Hyde is described by many a literary reviewer over the centuries as animalistic, radically self-preserving, and highly dangerous. It is my belief that our innermost selves which are controlled by emotion and not critical thought represent the Hyde side of everyone. After all, most of us are a few IQ points away from the animal kingdom. Hyde can of course be brought out with the right dose of caffeine or liquor, but in many ways understanding that we as humans have an internal struggle that is neither schizoid nor even abnormal is to comprehend the competition between emotion and rationality.

Marriage proposals, valedictorian speeches, funeral eulogies and other forms of congratulatory, introductory, or conclusive events are the times in which to express emotion as an outermost facet. Unfortunately, we are consistently connected to stories in which people utilize passion before principle. We see murder and love intertwined, scandal, compassion lent to evil, and evil lent to compassion. For us, as a human race, and not just those of us with Tourette's Syndrome, I adamantly suggest the acknowledgment and respect of emotion as a driving force to a great endgame, but not the sole decision maker when we have so much intellect as even the most basic of humans. I feel that there are portions which reflect the outermost expression of my emotion where I speak from my heart, and there are other stretches like the current passage that rationalize the issues I and we all have within us. It is my hope that the book at hand is microcosmic and almost an imprinted mediator between the head and the heart.

Regardless of what happens in our heart, our heads, or our pants, the only way to begin the action of whatever decision is made is through the hands. I had a terrific history teacher my senior year of high school named Mr. Jeske. He was a remarkably intelligent, compassionate conservative surrounded by New York liberals transplanted to Boca Raton and their offspring who believed in their own entitlement because their father drove a Bentley. Mr. Jeske intelligently alluded to the difference between lawful and unlawful action, by swinging his fist like a pendulum. He explained that so long as his fist makes no connection with the face of a student, he is legally allowed to move his fist, but once he purposefully makes a strike on a peer, he has violated the law. I like to think of emotion as something along the lines of Mr. Jeske's fists. Emotions, dwelling in our hearts and coursing through our brains in electrical impulses more complex than even the remarkable cosmos are all acceptable until they are acted upon, and then once they have been exposed through the tongue or the hands, they then are digested and interpreted by society. For example, when my ex left me I had a few choices. I could get irreparably drunk and die a Poe-like death, I could kill her, or I could work to better myself and understand the circumstances that led to our failure, moving forward and priming myself for the next opportunity to arise. Now, suffice to say I certainly did take some Edgar Allen Poe like writing methods to heart, under the influence at certain points of this book, but when we realize how insignificant we are on this vast blue planet, and just how many minutes and days and years we are given and how much opportunity we will present to ourselves and be presented, it becomes easier to step outside ourselves and grow up.

The beauty of humanity only being able to use a fraction of its brain, given the hypotheses of telekinesis and telepathy as possibilities if we used all of it, is that people see us but they never know what we're thinking. Imagine if every person on earth acted upon their darkest instincts and emotions. We would be in a post-apocalyptic waste where everyone had a target on his back. Thankfully, I haven't really gone out of my way to make anyone hate me ever, so I'm pretty sure if you polled the local populace on their opinion of me, the only folks who truly vilify me would be anyone connected with my ex. That's fine, as I don't believe in "velvet divorces." If someone finds it worth taking you into their homes and hearts, and then casting you out to the world like common waste, then why should we treat them like anything else but a force of expulsion that for their own personal interests enact emotional harm to us? I don't really like to have tentative, touchy relationships with past friends or lovers, and thankfully my list of lovers and friends is short enough to where I don't have to walk upon eggshells every time I step into public. But for me, the Snake Plissken chaotic neutral type character is something false and unreal, only existing in Hollywood fantasies. While I do believe that good and evil are not as bipartisan and exclusionary as someone like Tolkien might place parties in Numenor, it's easy to see that you're either with me or against me. While it is, in fact, frightening and coldhearted to consider someone a friend or foe, and not in between, consider the three types of interactions. The only time one is neutral is upon first encounter, and only if they have yet to hear any other opinion. Therefore, unless there is a blank slate, it is suffice to say that within seconds – based upon appearance, profession, and conversation, an opinion will be derived. Rather than wasting our lives being people pleasers, it is better to acknowledge who our foes are and find ways to lawfully circumvent them. If they are in a position of authority, such as a boss that you simply cannot please, find a new job.

I spent a large portion of my childhood dealing with kids who today I know realize were understandably ignorant to my condition, but when you're alongside the other nine-year olds and there are certain ones who pick on you for who you are, there are only a few solutions. Reasonably speaking, instead of trying to win these people over, merely ignore them, or avoid them altogether. Being picked on as a child in a classroom can make you feel alone on an island surrounded by typhoons of insults hurled with alacrity. When you're a little boy, it's a fight to resist the urge to tell a teacher or chaperone, lest you appear weak and frightened before your peers. This macho attitude is part of the human psyche, and it is instilled and bred naturally within us, long before we begin lifting weights, having sex, and loading firearms – the macho works. For a long while I did believe there were remedies to the bullying by winning them over, and sometimes your greatest adversaries the first day of school are your best friends by the last, but as is the case, there are many who would do harm to us at any age regardless of why or how we came to deserve such treatment.

Once we realize that everywhere we go there will be unlikable people who will treat us poorly, we can filter them out and spend the little time we have on planet earth with people who react to us and regard us as friends. Another valuable lesson my mother taught me was not to ever bother with someone who isn't going to benefit me in some way. Meaning, never tolerate an individual on a selective basis who will be parasitic. The United States is chock-full of parasitic organisms, also known as the unemployed, sapping the very life's blood out of us. We work, we pay, they eat and they smoke. Given the massive world population, there is a guaranteed chance that you will come across someone who understands enough of whatever intricacies and issues you have to call you a friend. Out of those throngs of people, there are some called family, some called best friends, and some called girlfriends. These are the people you should fight against your instinct to please. Always fight against parasites and vampiric dredges of humanity, those who would rob you of your money, your well-being, or your life. They come in all shapes, sizes, colors, and backgrounds. They are at the top of the towers in

Wall Street and in the underbelly of the Subway shaking Styrofoam cups full of dirty change. This law also applies to friendship. They are the rich, the poor, the black, the white, the Hispanic, and everything in between. Never discriminate and disseminate your friends and enemies based upon anything but merit. The ideal working relationship, whether it is business, romantic, or familial, is a meritocracy. Merit is what earns support and a paycheck, it is why friends are friends, and the common ground laced with merit and pride are the hallmarks of a successful friendship. Humans are much like animals, in that they are classifiable but in many ways beyond just our appearance and biology. Too often we base our societies upon colors of the rainbow and floating men in space dictating family values on antiquated scrolls.

The moral of this lesson, is that assholes are assholes and they should in a perfect world, be culled. Unfortunately, the world is imperfect, and until we can find common ground in our imperfections, we will not find friends. We can't exactly pray for peace on a worldwide scale or ever expect it to exist, but what we can do is rationally manage conflict while deciding whether a relationship is worth it or not. Let us usher in a new age of Capitalistic meritocracy, a world beyond one where I am Anthony with Tourette's or Tony the Jewish looking kid. A world where

I am known for something I have done, whether great or evil, is what the world has known me as. It is my hope in my lifetime we are able to simplify the worldview we have around others and bring it to a more intellectual level. In doing so, we will avoid provocation by avoiding harmful individuals as a whole. Let us not waste our love on those who would abuse it, and while seeming more callous, managing our lives to a level in which we reduce conflict in our interactions to a minimum, while surrounding ourselves with helpful and healthy personalities.

THE DATING CHAPTER

Likely the second most miserable part of living with Tourette's after getting dumped is dating. After a breakup, our security and certainty is shattered by someone we once called "lover." And for many of us, the same questions loom afterward as if we were normal: "What went wrong?" "When did it start?" "Why is this happening?" With Tourette's, we have the obsessive accentuation of regret tied into our already self-destructive thoughts. So why then, if getting dumped is the worst of all, is the building of a new romance the second worst?

Let's think like an Israelite, for a moment. Twice, on the holiday (or mourning day) of Tisha B'Av was their remarkable temple destroyed. Twice, on the same day. After all that work from the first foundations to the great and beautiful constructions that gave culture to the house of the God of Abraham, within seconds these two temples were razed. In many ways, this is the grand fear of dating with TS. For many of us, our consciences are a bit less inert than the average bonehead boyfriend or girlfriend. For us, we are well aware of every word, every text, every smile, as a solitary brick. If rejection, as all men fear, is the result, then unlike womanizers who are capable of moving to the next like nothing happened, we ruminate on one date gone wrong. Even a single drunken interaction with a lady we just met will resonate in our skulls like a forever humming, always taunting wasp in the back of our cerebellum. So while like anyone there is a considerable investment, physically, monetarily, and most importantly, emotionally, in a new relationship, for us, we are hinging on so much more than just free liquor and kind text messages and banging. For us, we are waging a bet that includes our confidence, self-image, and altogether our well-being for a longer than anticipated time.

For some time now, I've been single. One year on September 8th will close the best and worst 365 days of my life. So much has been built and grown as a result of my fallout with my ex, and even though she's likely moved along through a palette of different Crossfit cult womanizers, I tend to view my sexuality and my emotion as something that never becomes separate. So many men and women are able to speak of and engage in meaningless, senseless sex for the sake of sating a weakness. Besides the physical benefits of sexual interaction, there's the feeling of being wanted and needed in the most carnal way imaginable. So while men and women across this nation and our planet bang each other for a cheap thrill, this is something that is impossible to occur in the mind of someone like me.

People are so ridiculous, they want a Jordan almond when they know the key to their health is a plain almond. Don't ever ask me to sugarcoat a damn thing. My friends from rugby told me I should get on PBS and do politically incorrect brief PSA's. This was spurred by my blunt statement to a young lady who was single at the time: "Don't accept a drink you haven't watched get made. You might get molested." I could've been kindhearted and walked on eggshells, but for every girl who's ever been drugged (I know quite a few), they might've appreciated my bluntness and vigilance. They let their guard down, and without protecting themselves, they assured themselves that they were around safe company and were near a haven.

We have to treat planet earth and our contemporaries as potential evils, and potential goods. Just because you're nearby a group of friends, or in an environment familiar to you, doesn't mean the chance for harm isn't there. Sometimes on off days at the bar (non-college, steamy body-heat festival nights) I like to show up at peak hours and people watch. I see more bimbos putting themselves in regrettable situations every day than I think I saw for years. They're so dumb. The problem is, people want to be amicable. They don't want to be cynical, and it takes some dramatic, hurtful event for them to become wary and protective of themselves. For years we skated around the idea of radical Islam reaching our borders, and it took 9/11 to wake people up.

Another fine stereotype about men I've brought from my politically incorrect pulpit is about guys with neck tattoos. I used to frequent a small bistro in Coral Springs with my favorite ex. Some juiced up bodybuilder used to go in there. He was such a jackass. I told one of the girls who worked there to never date anyone with a neck tattoo. She told me she was three months pregnant from a guy with a neck tattoo. Well, last I checked the baby was healthy and he was beginning a fifteen-year prison sentence. Hate to say I told you so. I've never seen, besides musicians, performers, and athletes, a successful person with neck tattoo. Unless you're the CEO of some cagey nightclub conglomerate, you'll be wearing turtlenecks to every shareholders meeting, or you just won't be there because you were dumb enough to get a neck tattoo. I have a fairly large tattoo on my right wrist, which was dumb, but I'm in a youthful industry and have the benefit of a nice set of dress shirts.

In many ways, the victims of date rape that I know (there are a few, whose confidentiality is paramount), can equate their first and hopefully final encounter with a douchebag molester as South Florida treated Hurricane Andrew. Hurricane Andrew molested the hell out of South Florida. The brunt of it struck a bit south of my home, but the message was clear. We needed one bad storm to kill a few people and destroy a few buildings before we were prepared. So when the outrageously powerful Hurricane Wilma approached, despite it being poorly forecasted, South Florida had Andrew under its belt, and with it new building codes, newer buildings, protective emergency procedures, and a booming shutter industry. I compare date rape to Hurricane Andrew, because it's the initial casualty of one's innocence, body and spirit, that cause the vigilance to spark. It is my wish throughout these pages to prevent your proverbial Hurricane Andrew, whether it comes in the form of a date rape, arrest, or similar altercation. Hurricane Andrew was to Florida what Sandy was to New York, so you get the picture. You have to view the world through blood-colored lenses, not rose-colored. Meaning, always anticipate the utmost cruelty from someone you haven't met. Let the common man prove his amicability. Let their good-nature earn their keep, instead of allowing their subterfuge conquer you outright. In Fort Myers, there are so many damaged goods that I am sincerely hoping as a success behind this book that I get to travel. Perhaps I'll meet an angel with Tourette's with a wonderful frame for childbirth, and we could be the progenitors of a master race of Tourette's children. I digress.

A one-night stand to me is like a dirty bomb. The initial explosion is scary, but the true damage is the fallout, the corruption of air quality, the cancerous alphas, betas, and gammas ejected into the civilian populace. While "normal" individuals like my ex or my most recent partners in copulation can get their dose of the male anatomy and move along like it's a fast food line, I cannot, and will not subject myself to being used as a pawn for someone else's insecurity. Sure, sex is a wondrous feeling, but I can't just do it to do it. This isn't a Nike inspired workout. People who require sex for security are doing it for all the wrong reasons. Now, it's not my place to tell people to be modest, because I'm not preaching modesty. I don't care, and it's not in my control who sleeps with who, but knowing myself, I avoid meaningless sex. Sex is the closest anyone will ever get to me besides witnessing my death. Why should I reveal myself to just anybody for a physical feeling? That's what rugby and internet porn is for.

Another reason to avoid frequency in sex is the fact that so many women and men all across the world are now walking talking viral and bacterial vectors. Sometimes when I am approached by a girl that is a well-known strumpet, I try to imagine her as a giant protist with the flagella somehow straightened into two scantily clad thighs. I certainly don't want any of this to be interpreted as misogyny, as you can see I mention men in the same sentences when describing humans as STD plague catapults, but in many ways the woman is the prey – the hunted. Even in our biological design, the woman is in front of us awaiting our arrival. Men know this, they know that they are the pursuit force, the one with the wallet and the shiny shoes that has to earn his keep. For that reason, knowing my own sexual appetites, I tend to view womanizers on a higher rung than slutty women. My ex used to call this a double standard, but all a woman has to do to get laid is be a woman, a man has to try. In many ways we are the knight, and they're the damsel, running from their Parisian village razed by Burgundy. And in knowing my own relationship between biology and sexuality, I in turn limit myself, not out of morality or preservation, but more protection and reasonability. Women who sleep around, who make out with everyone, are not to be taken seriously.

This is the same for men. If people have no choosing power when revealing their deepest, most naked selves, then how are they to succeed in other more calculative issues? How can someone possibly be discerning in business and in life if they can't even keep total randomness from thrusting between their legs? For unconfident weaklings like many of the young ladies I am unfortunately forced to interact with in social settings, I see the same characteristic I learned to hate: someone who thrives off of cheap attention, using their only untaxed possession as a tool to engage in mutual satiation. So for the longest time, after finding out that my ex within a few days was sleeping around, I let her behavior result in an indictment of my relationship with her. Instead, I should have focused solely on what I could have done in the future when the next girlfriend comes through, instead of kicking myself over the past and watching her destroy my present.

After so many months of self-destruction as a result of her actions, I realized that it is her failure, and not mine that forces her to require such attention. Furthermore, and this thought took time – they can have her! There are two types of people that everyone finds to be remarkably exceptional but are everywhere, inundated in our general populace by the millions. Good-looking people and great musicians are everywhere, so none should feel too high on themselves. For me to criticize my ex or any of the other local slatterns would be remiss to ignore the fact that I did have a few mindless sexual encounters since my bachelorhood became a sure thing. I wouldn't call it seeking attention, more to satisfy a carnal urge, but I want to remain as impartial as possible given my perspective, beginning as a scorned lover on page one and ending this volume as a chuckling, smirking, stoned and moved on lover of livelihood. I just don't want my readers to think that I am attacking my ex and the rest of society without holding myself to the same standard, so if she ever comes around to reading this: a big "frig off" (watch Trailer Park Boys) and an apology that I wasn't more scathing.

DATING PART II

I would be a fool to write a book about suspension between the worlds of imploding Tourette's Syndrome and society without first recognizing my own failures, both as a driving force, and as a follow-up product of my breakup. At least the emotional trauma didn't render me impotent! Yet as she moves, like so many others, through the welfare line of sexual interaction, I have come to realize that the only thing more miserable than not being loved ever again, is loving someone like that.

So before I erect (and yes, I love puns, so intended there) my newfangled temple of romantic carnalities, I have to be sure I invest in brick walls and wrought iron fences, gargoyles and shadows, using every brain cell in its construction as an architect with remarkable insight. I have to defend it with my life's blood and my own honor, instead of getting engaged again to someone who is all sexy and no substance. If the adage quality over quantity is truth, then I would rather feel nothing for the rest of my life than feel wrong and unclean. It is my sincere hope that my ex doesn't take too much offense to the writings in here, moreover I hope she takes pride that her leaving me created such a beast. It takes a spark to make a wildfire It's got to be a feather in her cap to know that even though I became successful as a result of being left, instead of a drunk, cracked-out inmate like the spiteful wretch may have hoped, that it was her who created this, or at least lit it on fire. If she ever ends up reading this, I want her to remember that neither one of us were the villains here, I just have a much louder voice. And to everyone else, if she ever reveals herself as the ex behind the madness, leave her alone, let her be, and don't let the temporary suffering held over me become some tour de force where everyone hates her. It's not my intention to paint her as a villain, moreover she is someone that clashed with me and eventually turned me into a place where I either wrote a book or caused great harm to myself. Unlike so many before me, I have been unconquered, even though I struggle here and there. I never intended this to be a defamation of any of my previous relationships, however the struggle within that is the premise in study behind this book, coupled with the externalization of failure and success, is enough for me to be as harsh as can be with reason behind it

I don't want anyone who appears in name or deed in this to think I'm going after them. Moreover, they are a microcosmic character in the greater scheme of things, a mere pawn on the chessboard of romance. And because so many young women, more here in Florida than elsewhere I've seen, are damaged goods, I have retracted myself to a point where loneliness clashes with the human need for love in order to determine my fate. I love the idea, as stated before, of constancy. It's hard with so much energy and so many gears turning in my mind, to focus on one sentence structure, so having to manage sexual tension with multiple ladies is not something I seek or have sought. I think another part of my disdain towards dating as a whole is the fact that many of the girls I know have been with dudes that are so incapable of being anything more than a gym rat and lower-middle classman with maybe a bachelor degree that it turns me off of them. Perhaps I'm spending too much time at bars and not enough time at charity galas and libraries, but to me it's clear that promiscuity has become a blight on the human race. There are a large percentage of people I would never consider being near, not because of their looks or personality, but because of my perceived status of them as wandering, drunken, plague-bearers. Sometimes I do things that I cannot yet (and will never) discern is provoked by my TS or not, like shouting anonymously in my apartment at home, or seeing people exactly as they truly are. Maybe my cynicism is a result of my Tourette's imbuing me with some sort of ESP in detecting a sticky strumpet when I see one, but thus far my modesty has paid dividends. Albeit, if I actually tried to gather these ladies, I'm unsure of the rate of success I would actually have. I don't want to come off as some studly gentleman capable of wooing women at the drop of a hat. For every woman that finds me beautiful, ten will see me as a monster. A lot of this is due to my natural personality alterations thanks to Tourette's, but I don't use it an excuse. There is an eternal challenge with which I struggle – that of maintaining and understanding the relationship between Tourette's and my conscience and subconscious being. Shrek once explained to Donkey that Ogres are like onions, that they have layers. There is remarkable depth to this statement, and one of the many messages delivered to adults via the classic film. In many ways, my life right now is in fact comparable to Shrek's. I live alone, get few visitors, but am content despite there being a burning inside – an inner drive that calls upon me to be something greater than I am.

Shrek, like myself, is sort of the lion-in-the-cage persona, where all civilians in one way or another are intrigued, but most are afraid to venture to his swamp, fearing some swift retribution via a massive chartreuse fisticuff. Yeah I'm just like Shrek, and would love to have a Fiona to call my own, but not now. Nobody is right. It's better to be unwanted than with someone dreadful. I learned this the hard way with my ex, rushing off into her mystifying wilderness with not even a canteen for the journey, let alone a paddle. I will not fail again.

At this stage of my bachelordom, I would be remiss to say I wasn't enjoying the freedom, especially financially, but it's getting to be about that time again. Time to open the gates to my temple and admit one. I would also be an outright liar if I said that still, to this day,nearly one year later, the fallout of that dirty bomb breakup wasn't dramatically affecting the way I treat myself and others. My rancor towards most everyone is something I hide within, but with the absence of sex my carnal hostilities have turned towards others. My relationship with human sexuality has been an exciting ride (pun intended) but one with great trials and tribulations. When I'm in a situation where I'm positive there will be eventual sexuality, especially with a new partner, I salivate the same way a panther does over his prey. Now in no way are women comparable to "prey" given that I am an altruistic lover and ultimate caretaker of the physically weaker species. I could compare many aspects of my life to vampirism: my sleep habits, my war between love and satiation of intrinsic needs, my struggle between my own biology and transformation.

One friend of mine asked what it was like to be my girlfriend. I told her verbatim: "Like falling in love with Dracula, the consummate romantic and Casanova, who cannot get out of his own way both biologically and emotionally long enough to sustain anything but heartache." "Yet," I continued. "While I've made much ado about the 'vampires' who have tainted my worldview regarding love, instead of focusing on the draining aspect of fictional vampirism, personally the stigmata I bear is more akin to Dracula's needs than that of a common bloodsucker."

I believe there is a deep relationship between bloodshed and lovemaking. Oft times when I am at my most frustrated, following a long span of dryness in the romance department, my aggressiveness towards other men rears its ugly head: like a blood-starved vampire. Since the earliest days of time, sex, and violence have been as one – as evidenced by Stoker's Dracula, the phallic symbolism of the sword etc. I get the exact same feeling, from my head to the pit of my stomach, when I'm either going into a sexual or violent encounter. The watering of the palate and the thumping in the chest combine with the swelling of the biceps. My ribcage, rattling like wind chimes in some macabre display. Humans are more feral than they believe, and most so in mastering the war between their urges and their needs. Urges, being represented as something they want to feel or acquire, whereas their needs are the rational and proper answer to any of life's vast conundrums.

Wanting to feel needed is why women put out, and the lust for cheap thrills is why men accept. As a result of insecurity permeated by modernity, this type of dangerous interaction is as frequent as ever. Sometimes I had to stare at myself in the mirror and talk to myself like a private in boot camp, to will myself to interact with women. "Get your ass outta bed! Go to the gym, get a job, talk to people! You look like a walrus!" If you knew me, you'd have known that I was hardly an isolationist at any point in my life, but for a while I was dead to the world, a ghostly façade representing my former glory, like the shade of a slain monarch still wandering his golden halls.

Individuals have forgotten the sacrosanct beauty of earth, resulting in women more concerned with how they'll look on this boat in Biscayne Bay to their Instagram friends, than their time on the boat itself. Previously, I mentioned courage and the ability to reintegrate into society following a major ego attack. Recapturing that and building upon the foundation I reclaimed was the next phase in life. If anything, this book and this chapter specifically will serve as a primer for any prospective date. It's almost like an "Anthony Owner's Manual." There's a section for several little slivers of my life, beginning at such a tender age. It's a great use to have such a document, if you wish to date me. I am the most hybridized, complex figure I've ever met, but even with Tourette's and all of my issues and qualms one might have with me, I can be compatible with almost anyone. Part of being a gunpowder pinball in a dynamite factory is being able to adapt to society, instead of forcing society to adapt to me. Adaptation is the principality that drives certain species to further themselves and ensures the destruction of others. I have to be like water when dating, able to adapt to the whims of a lady, knowing that constancy is comfort for me and most anyone with TS. I have all sorts of nutty things I do, quirks, unpredictability, but perceptibility. Humans are the smartest, but most inconsistent species on this planet. Because of our intellect, our goals and dreams are so diverse that they make war upon one another, person to person, nation to nation.

My mind is a shrunken version of human history: constantly at war, vying for prosperity, respect, recognition, and love. Like most reasonable and survivable nations, I must hold prejudices myself when choosing a possible date. Cautiousness is the only way, after multiple failed relationships rushed into, where the only place of my caution was in the wind. I have the gift of time, but while my coffers swell, my biceps pump, and I advance in the adult world, my mind still longs for the simplicity of daisy-blowing-latte-sipping-candlelight-dinner love, and even though that is so cheesy, that'd be a great addition right about now. A lady friend that lasts longer than a month is a boron control rod to my nuclear reactor, and without it I am Chernobyl.

Yet, while human nature is individualistic, there are several consistencies with everyone I've known that has Tourette's in terms of dating. We are fiercely loyal, and I have yet to see or feel myself ever be tempted by the cheating bug. Sure there are attractive women everywhere, but what do looks have to do with anything anymore? Good-looking girls, especially in my age group, are like rats. They're everywhere, they're numerous, they chirp and chat and consume, and sometimes even transmit diseases. And while it may seem misogynistic to compare beautiful women to rats, men are one in the same, difference being I'm not interested in having sex with them. I'm not saying I'm a good-looking dude, but I've definitely gotten into better shape and cleaned up my appearance since my ex started calling me fat and I realized she wasn't joking.

Incredible loyalty to family, friends, and our lovers is a hallmark of a date with TS. I would take a bullet, or fire a thousand for my best friend, my mother, father, brother, and at one point my ex. Now I'd rather shoot myself in the foot than protect her from whatever ruffian bastes her with sweet nothing's like a quail in the oven. Self-induced harm was in store for her, but regardless when she was in my arms my loyalty and stewardship over our home and our relationship were unmatched. My best friend growing up, the guy whose mom was so involved in the TSA and he who was diagnosed simultaneously with me, was married at 19 and never once wavered, cheated, or even shouted at his wife. He accepts her imperfections, as I always have, knowing that from our very cores we are flawed creatures, and to many we are twitching, emotional, cursing monsters. Thus, the owner's manual comes in handy here, because if one more drunk girl asks me if I curse because of my TS I might lose it. I curse all the time, but it's because I was raised by a tough family of soldiers, sailors, and wise guys. I've never been afraid to educate the masses, with this book as part of the effort, but the wear and tear of the bar scene is something that shows.

Our second most showing quality is altruism. I try my best to give off a vibe that I don't care and that I have little or no mercy for anyone, but I'm not sure if I believe my own bullshit anymore. And even amidst all of this maniacal hatred for these pathetic souls, it's hard for me to walk into a 7/11 and not walk out with a hot coffee and fresh fruit to share with a hobo. I really do hate a lot of people, but it would take a dramatic turn of events for me to stop showing the world my love, from my years of volunteer efforts on Sistrunk Blvd. to helping old Jewish ladies across the street in Crown Heights, I try to believe I'm a mean curmudgeon but I'm really a teddy bear. The same goes for girls, or dudes.

DATING PART III

When some guys get their feelings hurt they lash out, sometimes even with violence, but I am one of the most forgiving and understanding people, much to my detriment. Now, don't see this as me highlighting the qualities and intricacies of myself, these are merely all pieces of TS and dating, and it merely has fallen to me to be a mouthpiece for us. I've never heard of any grown man I've ever met cheating, striking, or hurting his lover. However, as I've mentioned, the one negativity to our undying concern and blood-written loyalty is our propensity to go down in flames. My ex tried being friends after our fallout, but I couldn't bring her into my life again. The idea of having her sitting there eating my food in my apartment, sharing airspace and breaking bread that she forfeited was too much for me.

Therefore, when breaking up with someone with TS, do not be afraid, do not think our peculiarity is going to lead to violence or suffering, but know that a blow is being dealt that for many is an emotional death knell, Tourette's notwithstanding. Whether someone has TS or not should not factor into any relationship decision. It should never come down to a reluctance to begin or end a relationship due to our abnormalities. We see the world through a completely unidentifiable lens that in many ways will appear irregular, because it is. Yet the one thing that is consistent with at least everyone I've encountered with the disorder, is loyalty and altruism, and a general consistency in outlook for the relationship.

Many of us would work tirelessly to feed caviar (gross) to the one we call wife, would put a thousand civilizations to the torch to protect one woman, would save every penny to make her holidays special, and would sacrifice every bit of our own clothing if it meant keeping her warm.

Thus, at this point in my life, if I see a lady I like I have to combine the impossible – walk on egg shells while on fire. In many ways I've become a hellfire missile, bearing enough experience to know who is and isn't worth it. Therein our investments become a bit focused, leaving an all-or-nothing yield for our efforts. As ex-lovers and friends continue through the endless hamster wheel of drunken sex and pointless relationships, we invest all our eggs in that one basket, knowing that losing that basket is an opportunity worth facing and winning his or her love is the ultimate prize. Nobody enters a race vying for second, so why would I ever walk into a bar and try to bring home a second rate strumpet like I have so often before.

What good has ever come out of a one night stand? If AIDS, rumors, and severed friendships are your cup of tea, then spread yourself and your legs like butter on an English muffin. I prefer to watch from afar and investigate, using an algorithm caught between emotional complexities and realistic odds such as proximity, age, station in life and more. This scientific approach to dating has yet to yield a true girlfriend, but it has only been employed since I have become a single man once more.

I have had a recurring dream that I meet my lover, my wife, at some point following the publication of this book. Possibly because a lady is fascinated enough to read this and thanks to words on paper has a general gist to understand the Jekyll and Hyde approach to life. I really can't help at this point that I'm a man of extremes, and like any abnormality whether it's a broken leg, ALS, or Tourette's Syndrome, we have to live in these conditions. Many women, I've found, believe that they need to have some dramatic change in their lives to date me, as if I'm an incommunicable caged beast only there to satisfy their desires. That's dumb.

Dating someone with TS is no more or less complex than any other relationship. We might twitch a bit, and we might see and do things differently, but we won't wind up on the Discovery Channel. Dating a dude with TS is no easier or harder than dating any other jackass. For every guy with TS in a rough relationship, there's 1,500 recidivists beating their girlfriends, probably right now. The reason dating sucks almost as much as getting dumped is the same reason why building Legos can be so challenging as a child. Would you rather have a standing Lego sculpture kicked down after a year on display, where you can behold its remarkable construction and artistic splendor, or would you prefer to have it set on fire as soon as the last block is clicked into place? For us, a failed date and a breakup are the same thing, albeit the tragic emotion fallout is minuscule when a relationship has not yet been in full form for long.

Either way, we are the harshest self-critics of ourselves and tend to be very constructive and understanding of others. Without being open-minded to others, how would we ever expect teachers, parents, doctors, and lovers to understand us? A while ago, I dated this really cool blonde chick who was just too young and immature to sustain something special. We had a great bond, but she was seventeen and I was twenty at the time, so understandably she was unable to keep herself reined in monogamously. Yet, the first night we made out, my vocal tics were awful. Even though I had to separate my lips from hers to cough a tic into a pillow, the remarkability of her understanding after barely knowing me long enough to make out was something that stuck me. Thus, she, like all ex-girlfriend's has a nickname: my favorite ex.

Why was she the favorite? She was pretty, very bright, affluent, but from the very beginning understood everything about my tics and at the very end knew to relinquish her role in my life after many cardinal violations in sin. The fact that anyone would kiss me, let alone hold me and embrace me when my tics were that obnoxious, is something that will forever stick with me, and she forever has my respect.

And at this stage, the hellfire missile I have become is an unstoppable force of romantic animality. While I have the presence of mind to quell such heat-seeking love in lieu of a date being overwhelmed, it doesn't mean that in the deep, dark, recesses of my mind I am not ruminating upon every possible outcome in a way that Stephen Hawking might run some fifty step algebraic conundrum from the seat of his chair. In many ways, despite interactivity and socialization, the complex pontifications occurring in my mind versus the discussions and dates I embark on is comparable to the voltage in your wall to a thunderbolt.

So many times I venture to express myself, only to pull back at the final bell in fear of one misunderstanding of my feelings. Despite those of us with TS having emotional and physical manifestations that are irregular in nature, we are capable more than most others at looking through every lens at every situation pragmatically, almost machine like.

This explains my complete distrust in the dating process, and the reservation I show despite my longing to feel loved and needed. I likely won't have a meaningful girlfriend for a very long time, but after so much suffering, it seems as if entering something on a whim like my previous failures would only be re-embarking on that trail that's been blazed and felled many times over. Better to be alone than suffer in company. This is also the difference between sluts and womanizers, and husband and wife. Why would I ever base my sexual construct around the omnipresence of big-breasted millennials when I can wait it out and find one worth keeping? These former, as mentioned in the previous sentence, represent the history of my dating life, and not a tale I wish to repeat.

I love the consistency, the cuddles, the feeling of being wanted, needed, held and loved, more than anyone knows, but to rush into a foolish new venture would be to put my eggs in a basket that has yet to be woven. I would be letting each oblong representative – my money, my time, my heart, my head, and my blood be metaphorically dashed on the ground and fried in the dirt and burning hatred that results in an unclean severance. There's a word for an idiot who makes the same mistake twice, and that word is Democrat. I bet you all expected me to say "my horrible ex," or "bimbo," but I figured it'd be a great opportunity as we near the end of this section to break the heavy prose you're reading with a quick swipe at an unsuspecting political foe.

I also don't believe in a "type," (unless Sandra Bullock has a Tourette's Fetish). Because by identifying a "type," one can immediately sequestered romance or the possibility of such, away from oneself. Sure, my ex was a dingbat who thought I should skip the squingili and our family time to go to church on Christmas Eve (gasp!) and maybe this is a dreadful example, but oft times we are attracted to those who are very different from us. I was fully willing to take our future children to the house of God even though I feel the hypocrisy in my bones each time a self-proclaimed Christian prostrates herself before me. In many ways the dirt I feel afterward is less about the act and more about the vilification in God's eyes if his texts are true to his sentiments, which we have zero idea of actually knowing.

I think if you look at the law profession in general (sorry dad) you'll notice a lot of married couples within it. Perhaps the very reason why litigious professionals marry is the same reasons so many of them are self-centered themselves. I have never seen a more arrogant statement as the "I've got a pen and a phone," shebang, but this is merely a half-witted sentence version of what makes marrying or dating "your type" a possibly negative union. This profession has given rise to folks like Johnny Cochran and Benjamin Crump, and made courtroom superstars out of guys who help famous murderers get away with it, then rush to the same courtroom to chide others for murdering someone they were fond of.

There has to be in many cases, especially for a man such as myself with my conditions, some common recreational ground suspended by a mutual respect of space, time, and romantic pragmatism, and inversely the doting and love that only my terrier has given me the past year. For many with and without conditions of the mind, this is a successful balance. I've always felt that my ex, for example, was (and probably still is) an alcoholic, who shortly following a breakup goes clubbing every night and usually ends up with a new guy in her bed and a prompt vomit session.

I am not isolating her as a special case, because this is a rampant and mass poisoning that many millennial ladies and gentleman engage in every Thirsty Thursday or whenever the liquor is cheapest and the music is loudest. my ex is merely an avatar for millennial women, and one that helped shape my worldview. For every drink that my ex sloshes between her lips, I oppositely prefer the calming cathartic effect of marijuana. For the longest time the only bond we had was smoking a bunch of weed and laughing at old episodes of The Office. I have to say, those were some great times, but to me "alcoholic and stoner" are like oil and water, and naturally they will separate and gravitate once their wild lives have sauntered. And at such an advanced stage in humanity, where drugs and liquor are so capably accessible and millions worldwide can define their lives' meaning by their substance of the day, it becomes imperative and necessary to define someone at least in part by their flavor of the week. In the same way our musical and film preferences can say so much about us, our drug and alcohol habits can too.

In fact, since the very onset of our cliques in middle school and moving forward, there have always been entire circles of friends whose primary bonding agents are drugs and alcohol. And even though she totally deserves to be chastised in a million different directions, I would be lying to you if I said I didn't have a circle of friends where the primary activity we engage in is smoking pot and watching television. So many friendships are made a million times better with substance abuse and miniseries. So for me to stand up like the failures of any of my relationships had nothing to do with me while pointing the finger at my former lovers for their failures only, would be a true harm to my self-image, my self-worth, and hypocritical. I would display the same hypocrisy that they showed whilst proselytizing me before their congregation.

In love, in life, and death, the first and foremost enabling agent for people to abuse anything — whether it's welfare money, their station in life, their good fortunes, or exploiting their bad luck for charity gain, is an absence of accountability. So from the very beginning, despite knowing that not everything was my fault in any of my breakups, acknowledging a rancorous severance as none of my own fault would be a bald-faced lie and a waste of printing materials and your money. The reason why people lie, cheat, and steal to and from their loved ones is their lack of discipline and respect for each other coupled with a disregard for accountability.

Accountability is the reason why Mumia Abu-Jamal should be decapitated, and is the reason why relationships such as my mother's and father's with their current spouses have been so successful. At age twenty-five and up, there's an added dimension to romance that includes things that Bob Marley would call superficial, but are as real as it gets. His religion caused him to be killed by his toe, which to me is offensive and stupid. If my toe is the reason why I die, please dash this book in a fire and point and laugh at such a ridiculous circumstance causing my eventual demise. But at some point, there are things like transportation, money, career trajectory, ambition, and housing that come into account. At my age, which I previously mentioned as twenty-five, career trajectory seems to be the defining factor in that litany of materialistic but necessary evils to be in a successful 21st Century relationship.

This was also one of the reasons my relationship failed with my ex. I hope she can become something special without using her good looks to get there, because what attractive people don't realize is that they're more numerous than rats on the F train. I'm not the ugliest dude in the world, so there are a few things I can likely achieve with a wry smile and well-placed flirtatious quips, but being a sexy young lady only goes so far. Some of the ugliest people in the universe are the most successful, and some of the darkest, most evil people out there are in power across the world, and this realism was a disconnect that led to failure. Being attractive and horny can get you on Penthouse, but not living in one.

I have never been one to sugarcoat or paint anything rosy, leading my step-grandfather to jokingly nickname me "The Ambassador of Goodwill." I come from a family that has white collar crimes driving us apart, destroying what goodwill we had left in us, so I'll be damned if I let principle or religion or humbleness get in the way of building my nest egg. Because, no matter what young college longboard skating, Birkenstock wearing, dreadlocked hippies tell you, you need money, you need power, and you need a job to survive. They'll stop selling free love when their student loans catch up to them.

This dynamic isn't really part of the plan until the post-graduate eras of our lives. In understanding, I have been watchful and wary of my surroundings, trying to build as much wealth as possible, not out of avarice, but out of the necessity for a comfortable living. Most importantly is getting this into the eyes, minds, and hearts of people who might need a wake up call or a pep talk when they can't stop twitching. This book reminds me of the feeling George Washington Carver must have had when he invented the magical concoction known as peanut butter. The dude was born at the height of the Civil War as a second class citizen, and educated himself to the point where he saved the south from the boll weevil pandemic that crushed the monoculture cotton crop in his day with his work in peanut farming. Yet, whatever fiscal gain or fame he achieved must have been paled by the impact in knowing that in homes all over the world there was now an unstoppable, imperishable force that could sit in a pantry through a nuclear attack and still feed the whole family.

That's kind of how I feel about this book, in that maybe this chapter will provide insight to everyone, not just those of us with TS, as a realistic look into the complexities, intricacies, and unfortunate miseries of dating. It would please me more to sell one-hundred copies for a dollar than ten for fifty, knowing that my literary peanut butter was now slathered on the midsections of happy couples everywhere.

You've got to be a real schmuck at my age or older not to take fiscal and professional concerns to the table when you're arranging a budding relationship. We can look through the rosy lenses all we want and sing Kumbaya, pretending money and houses and cars and children don't exist, but they do and they're all part of our lives. The divorce records in America also prove that money and careers or a lack thereof destroy relationships. At our age, there is a general disconnect between otherwise compatible couples. At this point it's a make or break type stage where some burn out and some ascend. I hope, truly, that if I do wind up making a career out of this, that my potential mate finds me before my career finds its way to success. While the reassurances of entering a relationship with someone truly successful make me feel secure, it's also seemingly an added incentive for certain types of people to hinge on finance instead of romance.

This is the reason why at this point in my life, being single for nearly a year, my principal focus remains on my work, my physical shape, and the cleanliness of what's in my skull and in my home. This whole period of self-discovery culminating in this book will be a dramatic boon once I do in fact find someone I love and loves me back. If the grandest goal in life is a white picket fence (or black steel and gargoyles for me), a dog and two smiling children in khakis and Keds sneakers, then I must dedicate every moment in this dramatic, emotionally charged span of life into the preparation for the onset of new love.

Suffice to say, I'm not looking, nor am I trying very hard. I'm fully capable of bringing a girl home from the bar on $2 well nights, but reverting to the dirty bomb comes into play. I've had some one night stands since my breakup, and nothing is left but hollowness and unfulfilled desires still reaching out for truth in romance. Anyone can put his penis in something or someone and call it love, but the one longing I have more than anything is to make love again, instead of just banging. Yes, there is a huge difference between rum running rough sex with a sorority girl and making love. There's an emotional connection that's omnipresent when you feel, and even if this conversation is gross, it's truth.

The truth is gross, it's carnal, and sometimes it can really hurt, but I haven't made love in a long time, and it sucks. So if the American dream is a wife, a dog, a family, and a lovely bit of cash, then I am well on my way, but the ascension to happiness is only a sapling in a forest of groaning, swaying petrified trees. There's something so quaint and convenient about being in love, that it's something I've grown mature enough to avoid forcing at this juncture, but aware enough to know that to die happy is to die near those who love me.

In reverting back to the original premise that to have Tourette's Syndrome is to be completely inconsistent and persistently tormented by the incapacity to regulate our own minds and sometimes where they wander, it's easy to see that everything I've been doing is a big preparation for another single soul to rebuild the fallout from the initial detonation that spawned this whole document. I've spent my whole life under the influence of Tourette's planning for the next great thing, and trying to assure some semblance of security. Therefore, my argument that fiscal success is paramount to romantic longevity is as valid for someone with Tourette's as it is for anyone on this earth.

Consistency is a wonderful thing for us, and until a lady marches into my heart, the only thing I can do is make sure I look my best, feel my best, protect my family, and build a career worth being proud of. The self-interest is in no way superfluous or self-centered. If we cannot manage ourselves successfully, how can we manage the confluence of another personality through times of conflict and of burden? This is why I have plants instead of dogs or hamsters, because I am mature enough to know not to take a living thing into my home without lengthy self-assessment and introspective analysis. In many ways, our lives are a great trigonometric algorithm, in which we pick three defining principles to live by, and they all struggle for supremacy.

One of the defining statements of the Boy Scouts of America is "God, country, self," therein promoting a top to bottom dedication to community and service through faith. We all have one of these quips to define ourselves. Mine, as of now, would be "family, career, and love." In that order, which from year to year can be replaced or reverted to previous commitments that have phased out of or implemented themselves into this great life-defining triumvirate.

The issue I had, and that I have with so many females, is their complete lack of self-control or sense of place. Exhibit A are the lovely drunk slatterns that populate the bar I frequent, bobbing from man to man like a Frisbee and never being assured of their own success nor of their future. This complete lack of foresight doomed my relationship previously, both on her part from a career perspective, and mine from a multitudinous list of failures. I spent a long while in argument hurling harmful insults and malediction, only to see my testicles crushed, my hard drive broken with poems long gone, and my forehead split by an engagement ring. In hindsight, I probably deserved most of it, but getting into something so rapidly following each of us breaking up with our previous significant others (hers involving a domestic incident) left us searching and unprepared for what was to come. For six months things were smooth, until our skeletons twisted the knob and emerged from the closet, followed by disagreements over our religious freedoms and preferences, along with the aforementioned liquor barrages.

Today, August 16th, I have been nursing the granddaddy of hangovers. I recall the scene in Greek lore when Hephaestus the God of smithing crushes Zeus's skull to reveal the great relief, and Athena birthed from a historically bad headache. That's sort of how I felt this morning at about 6AM. Last night, I drunk texted my mom, explaining how much I hate liquor and how it's destroying my emotions. I went out with two gorgeous girls made up and dressed so wonderfully, and I'd like to think I have a chance with either one of them, as they both represent in one way or another some sort of compatibility, but I'm smart enough to know two things: don't mix liquor and meaningful conversations, and don't date girls who are vulnerable. Both of them are mature and intelligent enough to understand their roles, but neither are at a phase in life where I would want to tread water with them. This is something that I learned only following incredible heartbreak. That is why I wrote this book, because you can really take years off of your life dating someone who you approach in a vulnerable state. In today's twenty-four hour cycle of social networking fueled rumor mills, it's really easy to get caught up in dangerous speech. Which is why, at the one bar that I frequent more than any establishment, I avoid banging any of the bartenders at all costs. Even though the entire lot of them are attractive, exposing yourself like that to a legion of in and out singles who have eight hours on an off-night to talk about the shape of your penis or the psychopathy on your iPod I call music. Really, the majority of failed relationships or sexual liaisons are graves dug by the parties within them.

That's why in order to learn anything from failure you have to hold yourself accountable. It is my sincerest hope that those of us caught in the throes of Tourette's and its toll on our mental energy are able to take something from this chapter and apply it to their dating situation. There are thousands of words here that are likely some form of nonsense if read in isolation, and perhaps it's the caffeine and the still digesting liquor doing the talking, but there is no better feeling that the sureness of romantic and financial security combined into one tremendous relationship. To capture this rarity one must be self-aware, aware of his own interests, and aware of his lovers', all whilst combining these moments of clarity with the vulnerability and the omnipresent understanding of every failure.

My Dying Bride, one of the great Doom Metal bands of all time has an album entitled A Map of All Our Failures, which is a perfect way to understand why your failures in everything you do should never leave your mind and heart. If you glance over your mistakes, forgive and forget your enemies, and enable your friends to be advantageous and parasitic, then the absent cartography of your failures will in turn be your greatest of all mistakes. Take inventory of everything you've done right, and wrong to this point, as I hopefully have in this book, and remind yourself that nothing ignites a fire in one's heart like true love or true hatred.

These twin pillars of passion should fuel everything you do. I got in shape because I hated my ex-fiancé calling me fat, and since then amid patches of laziness here and there and the occasional bowl of ice cream, I've maintained a lovely slab of meat for a body. Everything I've done to this point has been to prove a parasite in my past wrong, and make her look like the loser in this quite deleterious divorce. The most important thing you can do when capturing these two feelings and channeling them as motivation, is to remember that hatred lights the fire, but only true love and kindness can keep it aflame.

FINAL ADDRESS

Have you ever read The Art of War? The age-old discourse on ethical and effective warfare could fit in the breast pocket of many shirts. Its length is not a concern, and in many ways makes it special. The fact that so much experience is captured in such a small encapsulation makes every line that much more concise and intrinsic to the greater message.

That was sort of the design that was in mind with the book in your hand. I didn't want some verbose diatribe outlining every moment of my life from my first tic to the one I just had. I'm twenty-five years old, how much can I possibly gloat about? It's like how Victor Cruz released a book about himself after catching ten touchdowns. How boastful! By 2009 I got pretty sick of listening to Obama talk. It wasn't so much the fact that we disagreed on pretty much everything, but everything he did was to address his own ego and boost his image via outrageous amounts of speeches. It got to the point where I just wanted him to shut up and figure out what he needed to do to actually fix something instead of just talking about it. Terror problem? Racial unrest? Let's have a speech! That'll solve things.

This book shouldn't have taken you long to read at all, but going back into the pages and thumbing through certain passages that you may find more powerful, confusing, or even comedic than others will validate the length of the book here. It doesn't need to be any longer than what it is, because these are lessons that you will learn from me. These lessons are ones that I learned the hard way, and in reading the details of my mental operations, the reader might have a glance into the blueprints of my mind, and therefore reflect upon his or her own subjectively from afar. Really, this is just a few fun stories, some dark, ominous outlines, a few motivational cheesy moments here and there, but more than anything a discourse on creation, destruction, and getting along with society knowing that I am so different despite my appearance as a member of the greater normality. There is solace in knowing that while I appear as one of the rabble, I will always stand apart. There is nothing wrong or upsetting about TS, but it can get in the way of what those with TS want for themselves. Reading my book won't quell any tics and it certainly won't make them worse, but it may open eyes to the interactions between emotions driven by TS.

Since tics are really quite inevitable, I wanted to reflect more upon the emotional and reactive side of the triad and encourage readers at every step of the way to learn from my errors in judgment and the heartaches with which I have made such an unfortunate reality in my life. I would love more than anything to hear from anyone, and I promise no matter how big this volume ever becomes, I won't be having any publicists answer emails and letters. Moreover, I would prefer to take longer to address them all myself. Remember that everyone is special in every way, and no one is less "normal" than anyone else. In fact, all of society has one thing in common: none of us are normal. So when I went through the tear jerking magma conflagration that caused the initial forays into the written word which eventually became a book, I remembered that my mother went through a thirty-year deep marriage before losing her husband, my father, or that my Pop Pop went the final years of his life without his only wife, and that there is someone in Africa working long hours in a mine who is more exhausted than I am, or that there's somebody right now rotting in an Iranian prison for being Christian. Then and only then do I realize how insignificant my gripes truly are. Pain and suffering manifest in many forms, and despite their near omnipresence within my spirit and body, I treat them like any other health issue that someone may have. Diabetes, cancer, artificial limbs, and so many other handicaps are much worse than anything I have ever suffered.

I am humbled by the bravery of some of the people I have come in contact with – soldiers, children, the aged, the sick. Thus, my days of the "pity party" are over. I taught myself to live with sorrow as I have learned to live with tics. Sometimes my elbow pops out, or my head hurts, or I clear my throat too much in a quiet room, but I never truly pay too much heed because I made it routine. Emotional disappointment should never become routine, but as long as you're living with any misery or discomfort, the only way out is to accept what you're feeling and find a way to meander through the shadows to the meadows beyond the eyes of deceit and pain. It's not a movie, if you're in a rut you're in a rut and no deus ex machina is going to escort you out of there to roll the credits.

So I hope you got your money's worth out of everything, and maybe even a chance to hang out with me sometime. Remember that I do not know everyone's issues at home, TS severity, or monetary situation, but I know that there is one thing in common with all of us possessing Tourette's Syndrome. We are strong, we are one, we are in this together. If one of us goes down, we all go down after them. If one of us stumbles, we will lay our bodies down to catch their fall. Find what is dear in life and grow to love and preserve everything that is important.

If there weren't such fundamental differences between my ex and I, we may be married today. Yet, the past is the present until you let it go. And for us it's damn hard to let the past go no matter how bad we want to. Remembrance of struggles past is extremely important to ensure survival. The memories of suffering I have endured many times before is what enabled me to write this book. Reaching back even a few months for how I felt at that time is like gazing through the eyes of demonic presences, taunting my very spirit. Yet, expelling the ghosts within and emerging as a man, or a woman when the time comes to blossom as an adult is the biggest step in everyone's life. I have only lived a quarter century and have so much to learn. I have been humbled by all this hurt and have promised myself a million times before that I will do the right thing in the future. I can safely say that almost every mistake I outline in detail in this book was as important to my well-being in the long term as it was to my short term emotional combustion.

Yet, amidst it all I kept everything in order, like gathering a spilled bushel. Pain comes and goes, tics come and go, as do lovers, enemies, friends, professors, and so many other human entities. The past is the present until it is accepted and allowed to leave your being. Scars both physical and underneath are just a reminder of a fight survived.

Please join me in finalizing the journey which we have sailed upon together by reflecting on what I have written. Writing this book was as important for my own spirit as it was yours, as sometimes my lightning fingers and Cuban coffee can reveal what my subconscious meanderings are without even searching for that deeper layer. A successful relationship, or human being in general needs three things: heart, brains, and courage. Without such important qualities, the Tin Man, the Cowardly Lion, and the Scarecrow would never have been able to work alongside Dorothy to escape the clutches of the Wicked Witch and realize their dreams of a peaceful Oz. And in the end, the revelation that defines the film is that they had these qualities the entire time, and only found them in times of peril.

Metaphorically speaking, this is a great way to weigh your quality of person. Ask yourself if you have these three qualities. Are you being honest with yourself? Honesty is the best medicine. It is why I am loved and hated, not anywhere in the purgatorial middle ground amongst public persons. If a woman is a graceful beauty I will tell her, where inversely if I think someone is being a jackass I'll notify them promptly. There are few things worse than uncertainty but filling our lives with bandages and not complete rebirth is just another path to disaster. my ex was a Band-Aid, and ripping it off that still open wound was infectious for a time. A gauze wrap and Neosporin can stop the bleeding, but healing comes from within. Please get a hold of me if you can. I've got your back as long as you promise me you'll first and foremost look after yourself.

This is as much a collection of my own sorrows and pleasures as it is a way to show the light to families with someone with TS and disorders along the spectrum. View it as a storybook, a science book, an intellectual treatise, but please do one thing in constancy no matter what shelf this book winds up on: take morals and lessons away. Learn from the pit of my chest and the abyss that was once a hemorrhaging heart. Only you can conquer your greatest of adversaries. In many ways I have, but my journey only has just begun. I am thrilled to begin my literary career with a book that will hopefully help many. I am proud to release these pages unto you, and hope for sure that sometime I can meet you. Perhaps you have a bachelorette in the family? I'm really a sweetheart, and haven't advocated for any negativity!

Just take it and shape the outcome of this book around your own value system instead of using mine as a basis for the readings. See how this compares to you, and how your personality manifests in comparison to mine. I wish you courage, honor, valor, pride, and most of all a few minutes free of twitches.

For love, learning, and labor,

Anthony Moritt

ABOUT THE AUTHOR

Anthony Moritt is an author and advocate for those who have been diagnosed with Tourette's Syndrome and other neurological complexities. His distinctive voice and passion for bringing to light the realities of this diagnosis are evident in his debut book, Mental Anarchy: Tourette's Syndrome and American Dystopia. From war and peace with family members, teachers, doctors and classmates to navigating the rocky roads of romance, Anthony's unwavering, fearless honesty is the foundation of his book — and his life.

Never one to shy away from a challenge, Anthony has embraced and openly shared numerous elements in his personal journey so that others may learn and benefit from them. He has an unflinching view of life that is at once raw and unfiltered, as well as humorous and upbeat.

His perspective is both unique and identifiable. He presents situations, reactions and interactions that make his story universal, yet intensely personal.

Anthony Moritt is a powerful voice for the community. He is a presenter, blogger, writer — and someone who speaks from the heart.

Learn more at www.AnthonyMoritt.com.

Made in the USA
San Bernardino, CA
29 January 2016